COST STRUCTURE OF COLLEGE EDUCATION

COST STRUCTURE OF COLLEGE EDUCATION

By

Dr. Harjiv Kaur Sidhu

M.A. Ph.D.

Assistant Professor

Deptt. of Economics

Trai Shatabdi Guru Gobind Singh Khalsa College

Amritsar

DISCOVERY PUBLISHING HOUSE PVT. LTD.

NEW DELHI-110 002

Published by:
Tilak Wasan
DISCOVERY PUBLISHING HOUSE PVT. LTD.
4831/24, Prahlad Street, Ansari Road
Darya Ganj, New Delhi-110002 (India)
Phone : +91-11-23279245, 43764432
Fax : +91-11-23253475
E-mail : parul.wasan@gmail.com
discoverypublishinghouse@gmail.com
web : www.discoverypublishinggroup.com

***First Edition:* 2011**
ISBN: 978-81-8356-878-4

Cost Structure of College Education

Printed at:
Shree Balaji Art Press
Delhi

Preface

The major resource of every country is it people. So long as this resource remains underdeveloped, all other resources of the nation would also remain underutilized. It has long been accepted that education affects society and gets affected by it. It is critical to know more about this reciprocal relationship, if educational planning and development is to achieve the desired goals. Education is viewed as a potential instrument in development. The difference between developed and underdeveloped nations is not on the basis of colour or on any criterion, but on the basis of knowledge. Today only those nations are developed, who have the knowledge power as compared to underdeveloped nations. Knowledge power is the determinant factor for progress. In today's economy the most important resource is no longer land, labour and capital only, but also the modern technology, available supplies of purchasable requisites, a favourable micro environment and an effective education system that determines the progress of a nation. Nothing survives in modern society without knowledge. This is an era of knowledge which comes through education. Education is very crucial for emerging India. It raises productivity, enables new lines of production and lowers costs all around. It is instrumental in pushing the production possibility frontier outwards in any given economy and it does so with little or no extra investment outside, apart from in human resources. Higher education is an important form of investment in human capital. In fact it can be regarded as a high level or a specialized form of human capital, contribution of which to economic growth is very significant. It is rightly regarded as the engine of development in the new world economy. The contribution of higher education to development can be varied: it helps in the rapid industrialization of the economy by providing manpower with professional, technical, and managerial skills. In the present context of transformation into knowledge societies, higher education provides not just educated workers, but knowledge workers to the growth of the economy. It creates attitudes, and makes possible attitudinal changes necessary for the socialization of the individuals and the modernization and overall transformation of the societies. Most importantly, higher education helps through teaching and research in the creation, absorption and dissemination of knowledge. Higher education also helps in the formation of a strong nation and at the same time helps in globalization. Higher education allows people to enjoy and enhance life of mind, offering the wider society, both cultural and political benefits. This work is an attempt to analyze the cost of college education to evaluate and guide the resource allocation decision and utilization pattern. In the context of college education in Punjab an attempt has been made to explore the broad structures of college education. The study is composed of six chapters. First chapter is a comprehensive introduction to the whole work. Second chapter deals with the theoretical and empirical evidences related to the topic. Methodological issues have been elaborated in the third chapter. Structure of education in Punjab has been presented in fourth chapter. Analysis of cost of college education, its components and recovery system has been done in the next chapter. The last chapter sums up the conclusions and jots down the policy implications.

Harjiv Kaur Sidhu

Contents

	Preface	
1.	Introduction	1
2.	Review of Studies	6
3.	Cost of Education: *Conceptual and Empirical Issues*	59
4.	Structure of Higher Education	71
5.	Cost of College Education	100
6.	Conclusions and Policy Implications	145
	Bibliography	*159*
	Index	*171*

1

Introduction

Economic development is a complex phenomenon. Some theories attribute economic development to the labour intensity (Clark, 1975; Kuznets, 1963), while others attribute it to the capital (Heller, 1954). Modern economists emphasize technological change as the prime mover of economic growth. The new capital goods are assumed to be carriers of more advanced and efficient techniques of production than that embodied in the capital goods of the old vintage. Technological change here refers to the change in input-output relations of production activities (Mathur, 1963). The technological change requires not only right type of material capital but also an appropriate type and quantum of human capital. Thus, technological transformation of traditional economies into modern and developed ones implies different and much higher skills and knowledge on the part of manpower than currently prevail. In pursuit of technological progress education sector has received a considerable attention of both economic planners and policy makers. Both theoretical insight and empirical investigations by numerous economists have imparted shape and finality to the concept of human capital, education being the basic source of its accumulation

(Leontief, 1953; Shultz, 1960; Blaug, 1968). The success achieved in the quantification of economic value of education made both policy-makers and theorists euphoric in their accumulation of economic function of education and its pivotal role in promotion and acceleration of growth, imparting impetus to empirical investigations of the education-economy interrelations (Blaug, 1987).

The on-going phase of privatization and liberalization, has given way to indifference and skepticism about education system in general and the higher education in particular. Resources are often in short supply. There is an urgent need to maximize the efficiency of inputs in the education sector and thereby eliminate the wastage of precious resources. In fact, the frequent claims of education sector for a large share in national budget can be sustained only if the resources already invested are fully and efficiently utilized. There is a general impression that the resources already invested in education sector and thereby the available infrastructure is grossly underutilized and a lot of wastage of resources is involved. Various commissions have emphasized to obtain maximum possible output from a given level of investment. Education sector is faced with the challenge of raising effectiveness of utilization of available resources.

Expansion of the higher education sector over the past decades has out-stripped the country's financial and managerial capacities. As a result the system is characterized by high cost small institutions; unenrolled specialized programmes; under-utilized facilities and an unproductive use of physical plant and equipment. Hence the efficient management of higher education concerns not only with measures to reduce recurring costs but also with the recovery of these costs.

The current decade U-turn in the economic policy changes has left, or is in the process of leaving almost all the sectors open to hard realities of the market. Subsidized for decades together and nurtured in a planned economy and public sector kind of environment, like other sectors, education sector had never been prepared for a market-oriented approach. By plain economic logic, a market guided system requires a maximization of revenue and minimization of the cost. It is in this context that the economic analysis of cost and the cost recovery in college education is the need of the hour. The study is an attempt to analyze cost and cost recovery of college education by going to a disaggregate level.

Objectives

The main thrust of the economic analysis of cost of college education is to evaluate and guide the resource allocation decision and utilization pattern. In the context of college education in Punjab, the main objectives of the study are:

(a) To explore the broad structure of college education;

(b) To analyze the recurring cost and its components;

(c) To study the effect of ownership type, location of institution and size of institution on recurring cost and its components;

(d) To evaluate the recurring cost recovery and surplus generation mechanism; and

(e) To make the policy recommendations for effective educational planning and administration.

Methodology

For economic analysis of cost, universe of the study is composed of 206 colleges. There are 6,200 total numbers of teaching posts in college education sector in Punjab. Out of this, 2,154 posts are with the government colleges. For drawing a sample, stratified random sampling technique has been used. The sample size of the study is more than 40 per cent of the universe. For drawing the sample, the universe has been divided into three strata: government colleges, government aided private colleges; and unaided colleges. Out of the universe, sample drawn is composed of 26 government colleges, 42 private aided colleges and 22 unaided colleges. Thus the total sample size is of 90 colleges. Using a well structured questionnaire, through personal interview method, primary data has been collected.

Typically, as per economics, an industry incurs two types of costs: current or operational costs and capital costs. Operational cost refers to expenditure incurred on raw materials, intermediate inputs, wages, salaries, interest and maintenance. Capital inputs may further be sub-divided into working capital and fixed capital inputs. Items of working capital refer to raw materials and intermediate inputs, wages and salaries. Fixed capital generally constitutes durable goods such as building, machines and equipment which can be repeatedly used in production. These inputs have a life span of their own and depreciate gradually with use in production. Both fixed and working capital inputs constitute a part of the stocks that have to be carried forward from one period to another. Current inputs constitute flow of goods and services into production that are used up in the production process in the same period. In education no distinction can be made between stock and flow aspects of working capital. Expenditure on both is classified as a recurring expenditure whereas expenditure on fixed capital is classified as non-recurring expenditure. So the cost may be classified by these two broad categories: Recurring cost and non-recurring costs. Due to inherent problems in the measurement of non-recurring cost, much of the work deals with the analysis of recurring cost, its components and recovery patterns. In a passing reference, non-recurring expenditure has also been analyzed but the prime focus of the study is on recurring cost only. For economic analysis of the cost of education, the unit cost has been arrived using the appropriate methodology.

There is hardly any consensus regarding as to what constitutes the main output of education. Education output is difficult to be measured both technically and monetarily. Education is neither demanded nor supplied wholly with an eye on its economic value. But the economics of the subject needs exact identification and measurement of all products and by-products of the educational productive process. Education is multi-product industry. Most of the studies have used enrollment as a proxy for output for unit costing and have assumed that all students receive same quality and quantum of education irrespective of personal efforts and motivation of students and the level and nature of course offered and the type of institutions. Given the objectives of the study in spite of limitations, enrollment has been used as a proxy variable to measurement of output.

For analysis, primarily the tabular technique of analysis has been used. Wherever needed, it has been assisted with appropriate statistical techniques like mean, coefficient of variation, correlation, regression and analysis of variance.

Chapter Plan

The study is composed of six chapters. The opening chapter is a comprehensive introduction to the work. Second chapter deals with the review of studies. Methodological issues have been elaborated in chapter third. Structure of education in Punjab has been presented in fourth chapter. Analysis of cost of education, its components and recovery system has been done the next chapter. Last chapter, finally, sums up the conclusions and jots down the policy implications.

Review of Studies

In the past, consistently constrained allocations to the education sector have raised issues relating to cost management and efficiency analysis of education systems in the country. In this regard, the study of unit cost enables one to estimate the cost of operating the existing educational institutions from which one can have an idea about the degree of cost effectiveness or the efficiency with which the system operates in a given situation. This enables the policy makers, planners and the administrators to discover the gaps in the functioning of the educational institutions. It also reveals the determinants of the unit cost that may suggest alternative educational policies to be pursued in future. In this context the present chapter is aimed at reviewing the theoretical and empirical evidence on the issue. The chapter is divided into four sections: section first covers studies on measurement issues; section two covers the system-wide studies; next section deals with studies on cost of education; and the last section finally concludes the chapter.

I

MEASUREMENT ISSUES

Pandit's, H.N. (1969) edited work is a collection of papers on education. The papers have been arranged in five sections, being each section devoted to a particular aspect. Section I gives papers dealing with conceptual aspects of costing of education and empirical investigations. The authors of these papers have discussed the issue for identifying the components of educational cost and the causal relationship between various elements of cost and productivity of educational institutions. Papers in Section II discuss conceptual and empirical issues that arise in determining the internal and functional efficiency of investment in educational institutions. Papers in Section III, present a rationale and approach to investment strategies in the field of education. Papers in Section IV deal with problems of productivity of education policy issues. Finally Section V contains papers that review the literature dealing with the problems in the measuring of cost-benefits of education.

Padmanabhan (1971) has analyzed the issue justification of expenditure on education. The study attempts to analyze that whether the best use of resources have been made or not. The resources covered by the study are teachers, buildings and equipment. Further an attempt has been made to ascertain whether the expenditure on education in India is in tune with the stage of the economic growth. India is spending a low percentage of its national income on education, which is lower than that of some of the developing countries. Another important feature is that the expenditure on education by the government is usually more in the urban areas than in the remote rural areas due to a variety of factors. The expenditure on education incurred by the State government in India appears in the budgets of their agriculture, medical, pubic health and labor departments in addition to the budgets of their education department. Therefore, when we consider the total expenditure on education in a state, we have to take into account the expenditure incurred by all these departments. But firstly we have to make sure that the items of expenditure on education incurred by the education department and other departments are related to each other in any special way. The work states that after taking into account all such complementary relationships it will be found that in India primary education consumes the major part of the budget for education because of the growth of population. But the real test for judging the adequacy of efforts for any level of education is the expenditure that is spent in addition to paying the salary of the teachers. It is because the major item of expenditure on education happens to be the salary of teachers and administrative staff alone.

Anderson, Arnold (1972) has proposed that by capable mobilization of appropriate educational data, building upon its historic base in nation wide statistics on social topics, India can lead the way to some decisive answers about the part that education plays or can play in development: economic, political, cultural, community, or social. India has extensive data, in some instances, however only fresh tabulations of existing data will open a treasury of precious information. What India lacks is the spare manpower that possesses both the interest and the experience or instruction in processing educational data beyond the first step of tabulation.

Prakash, Shri (1975) has analyzed the problem of measurement of productivity and of unit cost in India. Unit costs in this study have been worked out at constant prices. Data relating to unit costs have been taken from government publications. Costs given at current prices have been converted into 1960-61 constant prices by making adjustments for changes in the cost of living index. But item-wise adjustments have not been done. The work shows that the productivity of the Indian educational system may be measured by the number of passes in an examination and the number of students enrolled in the first year of the given educational course. It shows that the teacher-pupil ratio of all grades and types of education has fluctuated over the period covered by the study. Changes in the pass ratios show a rising trend for all grades and types of education except the commerce education for which the trend is a decreasing one. Pass ratios of college education are greater than those of school education. Teacher-student ratios are also supposed to reflect the productivity of educational output per unit of labor inputs. Though teaching time constitutes the largest share of total resource inputs into the education processes, yet the share of other inputs is not entirely negligible. Teacher-student ratio, therefore, reflects labour rather than the total resource productivity of education.

The study reveals many features of unit costs. Unit costs are divided into two parts: direct-average cost per student and indirect average cost per student per year by levels and of educational institutions Total average cost per student includes both direct and indirect expenses. Unit cost per student per year increases from primary to middle and from middle to high/higher secondary schools. But the cost per student in pre-primary schools is much greater than that for primary and middle schools, which might be due to costly techniques and inputs that are being used in these institutions. Another observation is that a place in the colleges of professional education costs a little more than twice as much as a place in the colleges for general education. A surprising feature is that the unit cost per student in universities is much less than the unit costs in colleges of general education, it must be due to the sub-optimal colleges. In India a lot of educational expansion has taken place due to private initiative and enterprise. Study adds that the misallocation of institutions is there due to political pulls and pressures and also because of private initiative and enterprise. It is but natural that most of the private institutions have been located at places where some person(s) could arrange financial.

II

SYSTEM-WISE STUDIES

Jena (1980) has tried to define the terms and giving some policy suggestions to improve the quality of education so defined. Educational costs can be considered from two viewpoints: from the point of view of the 'producer' and of the 'consumer' of education: (i) the costs to the agencies producing education, i.e., educational institutions; and (ii) the costs to the consumers, essentially the families. Cost-quality relation being the focus of this article, the author has confined himself to the institutional costs. Institutional costs comprise two cost components: recurring or operating costs and capital or fixed costs quality of an educational institution may be defined as its effectiveness in achieving its objectives. Therefore its quality can be judged from its outputs. Since outputs vary with variation in institutional objectives, there can be no single measure of outputs and consequently of their quality. Outputs include all the residual learning skills, insights, attitudes, styles of thinking-all the developed aptitudes and capabilities- that a student carries from the educational system beyond what he brought to it, initially from home or elsewhere. Taking students coming out of an educational institution as its outputs, their quality can be considered from the variables as: (a) percentage of passing students in terms of divisions and distinctions secured; (b) the magnitude of wastage and retention; (c) The age earning profiles of the qualified students; (d) achievement of students in the domain of co-curricular activities like athletics, dramatics, debates etc. Returns to education are accepted as a measure of the quality of education. Tangible financial returns accruing from education to the recipient or his family is easy to be identified and objectively measured. "Rate of return calculation", even as a crude measure of quality of the educational outputs, takes into account the direct economic benefits only ignoring the social and cultural benefits. Even if we brush aside social and cultural benefits, there are some economic benefits, which can not be measured. Author concluded that the assessment of outputs must be made in conjunction with the inputs that go into the process. Inputs serve as an index of the quality of education. The major inputs are: (a) teachers; (b) range of curricula provided: subjects offered, areas of specialization; (c) instructional materials; (d) methods media, strategies and techniques of teaching; (e) student welfare services: hostels, athletics, health centers etc.; (f) physical plant and other facilities; (g) facilities for research; and (h) institutional climate. These inputs, when intelligently combined and processed, keeping in view the objectives, tend to ensure the quality of the output. These inputs constitute the system's cost, whether expressed in physical terms or in financial terms. But the attempt at measuring efficiency or quality of an educational institution in terms of 'what is put in' suffers from an inherent weakness, i.e., impossibility of judging the efficiency of two alternative combinations of inputs to reach the objectives. Since high correlation exists between some items of current expenditure and institutional quality, identification of these items and intelligent resource allocation to these are of crucial significance. Care is to be taken to identify the items as these vary from institution to institution depending upon their objectives, level of development, and priorities in planning etc. Most of our educational institutions are operating at in-optimal or sub-optimal level leading to under utilization of available facilities. An effective and optimum utilization of the existing facilities would considerably bring down costs without impairing quality.

In his study, **Ramdas** (1984) has made a cost-benefit appraisal of education expenditure by identifying costs in education and evaluating education benefits, in general and with special reference to Pondicherry. This study relies only on the secondary data relating to from various sources and covers a period of 21 years, from 1960-61 to 1980-81. One broad conclusion that has emerged from this study is that educational expenditure in Pondicherry has definitely made a positive impact on the citizens of the union Territory.

A report was prepared on the basis of a mission that visited China in June/July 1985 (1986). The mission consisted of Messrs R. Drysdale (mission chief), W. Middleton and W. Pierpont (consultants). Ms. Ann Orr and Ms. Wy leung provided assistance in Washington. The report looks at some of the key issues for china in the management and finance of higher education over the next 15 years and at options for addressing them in the light of recent education reform proposals in China and of international experience. It covers a range of topics including: (a) a review of Government plan for long-term expansion of higher education posed as three alternative targets for enrollment growth; (b) broad estimates of possible demand for and supply of high level manpower in function of different prospects for economic growth and structural change in the Chinese economy to the year 2000; (c) an analysis of the recurrent cost structure of conventional universities including the distribution of costs by category of expenditure; (d) the relationship between unit costs and size of emolument and policies on student subsidies and cost-sharing; (e) an assessment of current practices in the planning, design, utilization, maintenance and management of university facilities; (f) an evaluation of university systems of accounts for revenue and expenditure and of management organization; and finally, (g) an analysis of the financial feasibility of plans for developing higher education to the year 2000 under different assumptions with respect to internal efficiency and cost-sharing for university institutions.

A chief goal of education policy in China is to achieve a significant expansion of higher education. A strategy in pursuit of this goal would necessarily follow three parallel tracks: (a) a sharp increase in emolument in existing universities; (b) establishment of new universities; and (c) expansion of non conventional approaches to higher education such as polytechnics, television universities, correspondence, special and evening programs, and universities for workers, peasants and cadres. By the analysis of the recurrent costs in the operation of conventional universities in China the conclusions are: (a) on an average personnel-related expenditure accounts for slightly more than one-third of recurrent expenditure; (b) the student-teacher ratio in Chinese universities is low in comparison to other countries; (c) a significant component of recurrent cost in universities in china is the cost of operating student residences, as well as assistance to students, such as fellowships, subsidies and food allowances, to underwrite some share of out-of-pocket expenses of attending university.

EI-Hout's (1987) work deals with the following objectives: (a) to describe sources of financing higher education in Egypt and in some other countries; (b) to highlight development of higher education world wide and in Egypt; (c) to analyze public expenditure on higher education in terms of (i) ratio of public expenditure on education to GNP, (ii) percentage of the total public budget allocated to education and (iii) expenditure on education per inhabitant; (d) to find out the consequences of scarcity of resources on the quality of teaching in higher education; (e) to highlight the international experience about alternative ways to mobilize additional resources for education. The study concentrates solely on public expenditure on education. Private expenditure is excluded because of the lack of statistics. Education economists agree that higher education has undergone a severe financial crisis, a crisis that has forced some institutions to limit the development of new programmes and activities. Using the case study of Egypt, alternative methods to mobilize additional resources for higher education has been analyzed. The demand for higher education is growing in most countries, faster than the resource base to finance its institutions. Moreover, on the average, the education, being demanded, keeps increasing in price. Sources of financing higher education are affected, to a great extent, by the type of economy adopted by the country, i.e., market, planned or a mixed economy. Evidence shows that there will be increasing financial constraints, and in many developing countries the percentage of public expenditure devoted to education has begun to decline. Three main arguments are used to justify the role of governments in subsidizing education: (a) social benefits of education exceed private benefits; (b) equity and equality of opportunity; (c) economies of scale. Thus it is more efficient to finance and provide education publicly. The work proposes some alternatives as: (i) increasing fees of student housing; (ii) providing loans and selective scholarship; (iii) earmarked taxes; (iv) community financing; (v) strengthening the relationship between higher education institutions and enterprises; (vi) reducing unit cost by improving the efficiency and productivity of higher education institutions; (vii) unconditioned international aids; and (viii) making planning for higher education more related to social and economic development plans.

Hinchiliffe (1987) in his work is concerned with the diversification of funding and decentralization of authority to the lower levels of government. Calls for the diversification of funding and decentralization of control in education made with the simple expectation that total finances will increase and that the operation of such a system will be non-problematic. Since the most far-reaching form of decentralization is federalism, the experience and responses of nations organized along federal lines may provide useful insights into the question raised. The author has divided the whole discussion into sections. In Section II, the arguments in favour of federalism are described together with the potential problems or drawbacks. Two of these problems arise from the existence or development of sets of imbalances regarding revenues and responsibilities of particular levels and individual units of government. Vertical imbalances are those that exist between the Central Government and all the units of a lower level of government. Horizontal imbalances exist when the individual units of a particular level of government each have differing levels of resources relative to their responsibilities. In Section III, the principles behind the different approaches to reducing imbalances are discussed. Section IV is the data center-piece of the paper. For six federal countries-the United States, Canada, Australia, Brazil, India, and Nigeria - the experiences of financing the education system are summarized. Section V contains generalizations of the most important features of these experiences and their implications both for federal countries and for those either operating or considering systems of diversified educational finance, together with suggestions for further work. It has been observed that in most federal countries, states in general have not been provided with sufficient own-source revenue or automatic (constitutionally guaranteed) transfers from the centre to finance their responsibilities of the additional transfers, shared cost programmes have been common, particularly in the developed countries. Of the federal developing countries surveyed, only in India are shared-cost programmes (run by some individual ministers) common, though plan expenditures in these countries invariably require subsequent recurrent expenditure by the states.

Inequalities between states' own-source revenue per capita are wide in the developing countries. In countries where significant equalization attempts have been implemented (Australia, Canada, Nigeria), the emphasis has been mainly on non-specific block or general revenue grants rather than on sector or project-specific grants. In other words, in keeping with federal principles, successful equalization attempts have been based on measures aimed at allowing all states to offer similar services rather than on measures that directly ensure that those services will be provided equally.

Majumdar (1987) has analyzed the role of the Finance Commission. The broad conclusions of the work are as follows. *First,* once Finance Commissions are persuaded that they should use explicitly criteria of efficiency, manpower requirement, or social equity, they should begin to review the existing practice of leaving the deployment of grants to the absolute discretion and care of the state governments. The specific purposes, particularly those involving qualitative changes in the pattern of non-development expenditure, must be clearly laid down. It should be incumbent on the State Governments to follow faithfully even after the lines, particularly those that would earn them a premium in the Finance Commission's award. A great deal of suppressed internecine strife between the education department and the rest of the state government should then be unnecessary. Admittedly, the acceptance of the principle of assigned grants in this area would be fraught with political, even constitutional, difficulties. But it is difficult to see how qualitative changes in the government and in the financing of the higher education sector could be ensured in any other way. *Secondly* we must all learn to look upon at least some institutions of higher learning in each state as national concerns. By emphasizing the all-India or even the universal role of the universities and accepting as their recurrent responsibility the reform of the academic as well as managerial structures at the highest levels of instruction, the Finance Commission can yet be a positive instrument of educational change in this country in a way the Planning Commission can never hope to be.

Pandey (1987) has brought in picture some of the shocking conditions prevailing in our universities and other institutes of learning. Higher education is the basic tool for social transformation and national advancement. It is expected to train the best manpower of highest quality in all walks of life. Pt. Nehru dreamed higher education to stand for humanism, tolerance, adventure of ideas and search of truth. However, serious anxiety prevails among all sincere citizens that higher education is not catering to social expectations. Universities being the nerve centres of higher education are not in a position to discharge their duties adequately either due to their internal obsolete dysfunctional system or due to external constraints. Contrary to the expectations, universities environment these days has given us a social shock. Violence, threats, intimidation, and coercion that have no place in academic life, have been actively resolute to and a small-organized minority of misguided students is holding everyone to ransom, very often with the help of external anti-social elements. The uncomfortable position of universities is essentially due to shortage of good quality teachers who alone can maintain better standards of education. Lack of financial and other material resources and constraints of limited employment opportunities; too, affect the behavioral pattern of students in higher education. So students' participation in utilitarian researches is desirable as it would broaden their outlook and deepen their understanding. However success of any attempt depends entirely on the collective efforts of politicians, social workers, community, teachers and students themselves.

The study by the Research Division of the World Bank's Education and Training Department of World Bank dates back to 1987. The major objective of the work is to provide alternative policy options in place of the existing public financing of education in the developing countries. The work is broadly divided into two parts. The first part examines the theoretical aspects of under-investment in education, the inefficient way in which the public funds are utilized in public education, and the resultant inequalities that are created as a result of the public financing of education. In the second part the policy options, with concrete examples are given. Rich statistical information, which is a prerogative of the World Bank, is provided in the report. A novel feature of the work is that it elaborates analysis and information relating to certain specific points in the text. The work recounts that there is an over-all decline in the public budgets for education in real terms. Due to the paucity of public funds for the expansion of education, social benefits of education have diminished. There is no possibility of coming out of the constraints that stagnated government spending if past trends are allowed to continue in the future. Therefore, it is suggested that unless educational development becomes less dependent on public funds, countries will not be able to tap fully the profitability of further educational investments. The inefficiencies and inequalities that are reported as occurring due to public subsidy of education need to be redressed. Three policy options are given in the present paper as an alternative to the existing system: (a) recovering the public cost of higher education and re-allocating government spending toward the level that produces the highest social returns; (b) developing a credit market for higher education together with selective scholarships especially for higher education; and (c) decentralizing the management of public education and encouraging the expansion of private and community supported schools. It is suggested that an increase in the tuition fee to recover at least part of the cost of production of higher education would not affect the over-all emolument much because there is an excess demand for higher education in all the countries. The authors argue for liberal privatization and decentralization by loosening administrative and financial control by the government so that a healthy competition between public and private institutions may be created. It is not very clear from the study whether the improvements in the investment in primary education through re-allocation based on principles of financing alone would bring equality between classes and castes; when the elite groups are likely to benefit from higher education and the masses from primary education.

Varghese (1987) has made an attempt to seek an explanation for the observed pattern of distribution of resources for education, particularly higher education in India. The main argument in this paper is that under conditions of resource-constraints, certain types of education will be more affected than other types of education. It adds that the availability of resources per student in professional courses has gone up, and that in general education has come down. Consequently, the disparity in the availability of resources between general higher and professional higher education has increased, favouring professional higher education. Admissions to these favoured courses are generally restricted to students with better socio-economic background. The rewarding system in terms of employment and earnings also favours graduates of these very courses. What follows is an attempt to provide one plausible explanation for such a pattern. Resources for professional education, in terms of per-student expenditure, on the other hand, showed an increase. The maintenance of such a pattern of resource allocation helps to satisfy the pressures on the government to expand the system on the one hand, and to maintain the legitimacy of the existing iniquitous system, on the other.

The paper by **Tilak** (1989) has two-fold objectives: (i) to present a survey of empirical evidence on the role of education in economic growth, poverty and income distribution ; and (ii) to make a fresh examination of some aspects of the some problem with the help of a more acceptable specification and the latest available data. The first objective is accomplished by making an extensive but not necessarily an exhaustive, survey of the growing research in the area. The survey concentrated on: (a) contribution of education to economic growth; (b) relationship between education and agricultural productivity; (c) contribution of education to improvement in income distribution and poverty; and (d) public subsidization of higher education and its proven effects on equity. The survey also included cross-nation as well as micro level studies. In the third part, a fresh empirical analysis is attempted on the relationship between education and poverty and income distribution, using the most recent data, and with slightly improved specification, compared to earlier research. In the earlier research, mostly current enrolment rates were used to explain current levels of income inequality. But critics argue that education may have a lagged effect, and as such current levels of inequality could be explained with the help of past educational situation or current emoluments may explain only the future inequalities. It concluded that the following hypotheses are true: (a) As the literacy levels of the population and the emoluments in education increase, the proportion of population below the poverty level declines; (b) Education contributes positively and significantly to reduction in income inequality; (c) It is the secondary education that has a more significant effect on the redistribution of income than primary education; higher education has, in general, either an insignificant or negative role in income distribution; and (d) The higher the level of public subsidization of higher education, the higher the income inequality. This is true in general and also in the case of the less developed countries, but not in the case of the developed countries. On the whole, looking at the education-income distribution relationships, and the explanatory power of the education variables, it argues that "no income distribution theory can claim to be complete without taking the dynamic nature of the human capital into full account". Education not only influences development, it itself is influenced by development. It may be claimed that all types of educational expansion may not necessarily produce desirable effects. With increasing levels of emoluments in primary education, a gradual shift may be made towards expansion of secondary education. Increasing allocation of resources for higher education at the cost of primary and secondary levels may produce not only on unbalanced education system, but also regressive effects on income distribution.

Jayaram (1990) pointed out that focusing on the disjunction between normative expectations of education and the existent constraints on its structure and functioning has been postulated: "education seldom rises above the socio-economic and socio-political situation in which it is embedded". So this paper attempts to substantiate this postulate by reviewing our rich and wide experience in the field of policy formulation and programme implementation with special reference to higher education. In the field of education, it is observed that there is not any lack of diagnoses of the crisis confronting the system of higher education or its remedies in the form of rational policies. If the mounting problems point to the loss of vitality of the system, the experience of policy formulation and plan implementation hardly permit any optimism. But it is also important to realize that the development of education in the post-Independence era can hardly be understood apart from the socio-economic and socio-political context in which it has taken place. Since these contexts themselves manifest symptoms of a crisis, one can hardly expect a radical restructuring of education to take place independently of a simultaneous transformation of the socio-economic edifice. Hence, a successful policy of higher education, or for that matter education itself, has to be conceived in keeping with a vision of the kind of society for which people are to be educated. Only if the political elite are committed to such a vision and are willing to make the requisite sacrifices for realizing it can a policy be tailored to its needs emerge.

Dandekar (1991) has quoted Adam Smith wherein two changes in the system of higher education are suggested: one, that the salary of a teacher should be only a part of his emoluments, the greater part arising from honoraries or fees of his students; second, that the students should be left free to choose not only the college or the subject, but the teachers who should instruct them. If we can work such a system of higher education on these principles, it will make the teachers more accountable, the students more responsible and the expenditure more fruitful. Smith's chief indictment of the system of higher education obtaining in his days was that it was contrived, not for the benefit of the students, but for the interest and the ease of the teachers. The indictment applies equally to the present system of higher education obtaining in our country.

Dutt (1993) has discussed the overall scene of educational expenditure in India. Educational expenditure in India, as a proportion of GNP, has risen from 1.26 per cent in 1950-51 to 3.30 per cent in 1992-93. However this is far behind the target of 6 per cent of gross national product for 1985-86 laid down by the Education Commission. This is not only lower than that of developed countries but also in comparison to the rates achieved in some of the underdeveloped country's expenditure on university education as a proportion of total plan outlay is likely to be brought down still further due to the resource crunch. There is an increasing dependence on state support and private cost in terms of fees. The decline in the share of endowments only signifies a drying-up of philanthropy. The author also reveals that subsidization of education at the college and university level is much higher. Government is finding it extremely difficult in view of the constraint on resources to provide for additional seats in regular colleges and university departments. Therefore, the government opted for the open learning and distance education systems whose unit costs are expected to be lower. Government should make a determined bid to mobilize resources for education, the fees should be raised, and adequate freeships and stipends should also be provided so that weaker sections would not be deprived of the benefits of higher education. Since industry and business are the real beneficiaries of higher and technical education, they should be asked to bear a substantial responsibility for financing technical and professional education. Funds contributed by them for infrastructure development should also qualify for tax relief. An educational cess should be imposed on professionals who, as self-employed individuals, are the other major beneficiaries group of higher education. Central and State governments should give education a higher priority by allocating more funds. However the unfortunate fact of the educational scenario is that even at the secondary and University/higher education levels, the cost recovery is less than two per cent. Some states have recently taken measures to increase the recovery rate by raising tuition and other fees; however the overall scenario in the sphere of higher education indicates that most states lack the courage to raise the level of fees despite the fact that the bulk of the beneficiaries belong to the upper income groups.

Levy (1993) has discussed the different arguments associated with the privatization of higher education. The pro-privatization zeal that has spread powerfully to higher education must come to grips with contrary arguments, which research and top international policy agencies have too often failed to consider. After presenting a worldwide overview of private and public emolument tendencies, the paper concentrates on arguments with regard to the creation, finance and performance of private higher education. The emphasis is mostly on two developing regions: Latin America and Asia. The analysis in this paper provides little direct prescription for action, but it is not intended as a ringing call to inaction. Instead, it considers a number of factors that can fairly be labeled as problems of privatization. It is a caution against action based on belief, explicit or implicit, in the easy or clear-cut, provable desirability of privatization. In an age of privatization forever, the article should cloud the picture a bit. Of course, even the article treats the policy issues as simpler than they are in practice. One should realize that good responses exist for each of the problems raised here. Beyond those responses, however, lie significant counter-responses, and so on. None of this condemns us to inaction while we endlessly debate. Even pending further study, we have enough knowledge about privatization to engage in serious, conceptualized and detailed discussion and efforts rather than to rely excessively on the conventional wisdom of our time.

McMahon (1993) has considered the level and the methods of financing human resource development in the developing countries with some comparisons to the United States and to the fastest growing countries. There are many sources of inefficiency as well as inequity in education that then transpose themselves into the pattern of economic development. Many of these are rooted in the methods of financing human resource development. There are economic criteria that are relevant to finding efficient and equitable human resource investment strategies. The social rates of return to investment in education, especially in primary and secondary education, tend to be significantly higher than the rates of return to investment in physical capital in the developing countries, and in the US over twice the real rates of return to investment in housing. Assuming that the externality benefits of education exceed the cost spillovers, and that the contribution made by investment in primary and secondary education to reducing inequality in the distribution of income in the future is non-negative, there are significant efficiency and equity gains to be made in the

US but also in the developing countries by improving investment strategies. Beyond this, improving the objectivity and equity with which funds are distributed to the schools by State governments in the US and by the Central governments in the less developed countries and increasing resource recovery in higher education in Latin America and else where. While improving the targeting of financial aids through better means testing, are two specific additional ways the financing of human resource development could be refined. All of these steps in more aggressive use of standard economic financing and investment criteria would increase efficiency and equity in the nation's total investment strategy as well as within education, and thereby contribute to economic growth in the US as well as in the developing countries.

The study by **Mehta** (1993) is a debate on cost sharing and financing of education in general, and higher education in particular, and a policy package consistent with the overall objectives of socio-economic development is also suggested in it. The work is of the view that the question of the necessity and quantum of public subsidies in education, specially, higher education, has assumed significance in the context of the new economic climate in the country. The market-oriented dispensation aiming at thinning of the government intervention and shifting emphasis from long term goal of social justice to short term goal of financial prudence and micro-efficiency is feared to adversely affect government allocation to education at all levels. The author holds that the policy shifts like full cost pricing of education, dereservation, privatization and even commercialization of education are in the offing; they may be introduced without any debate. It recommends that at the school level, the current situation of subsidized government schools, partially subsidized aided schools and unsubsidized public schools may be continued for the present. At college and university level, fees should be fixed as a pre decided proportion of average recurring institutional cost of providing particular types and levels of education. An estimate of the average institutional cost may be obtained every five years and the fee structure be modified accordingly. This proportion may be raised after every two or three decades. The fees should be indeed for inflation and the growth in real per capita income so that the average burden of fees in real terms remains nearly stationary. The capital cost should be fully borne by the state/community. At times, if the local community is ready to bear this cost, such possibilities should be fully explored.

The work adds that instead of subsidizing on fees without discrimination, as at present or with discrimination based on caste, income or any one scalar criterion, it would be better to subsidize on interest. This is also required to see that the beneficiaries and not the recipients of education bear the cost of education. For this purpose, provision of liberal long-term loan facilities so as to cover a large proportion of fees and private expenses will have to be made. In fact, a revolving fund should be created.

Ansari (1994) in his paper has suggested some economic reforms that focus on reduction in government subsidy and deregulation of economic control which have significant implications for university development. It is pointed out by the author that the university system is highly subsidized to provide the needed manpower for the economy. The system has, however, not been able to ensure (a) cost-effectiveness of its programmes and (b) equalization of educational opportunities for different income groups of people. This has consequently impeded the national efforts to accelerate the rate of economic growth and ensure equitable distribution of benefits of development, since the influence of educated and trained persons on all the socio-economic activities is intense and pervasive. In order to rectify deficiencies in the system and to direct its activities in such a way as to improve efficiency and accountability of the system, the fiscal instruments are considered vital and effective. The mechanisms of resource allocation to different types of universities by various central and state level agencies are neither based on scientific norms nor linked to the requirements for teaching and research. This has, in effect, led to uneconomic use of resources and has contributed to inefficiency in performance of universities. Consequently, economic growth and social progress are adversely affected. In distribution of funds for higher education, the accepted criteria of equity and efficiency are hardly adhered to, as a result of which the costs of even comparable programmes of education differ widely and there is hardly any incentive (disincentive) for better (poor) performance. The element of competition among the universities is therefore lacking. To remedy the situation, alternative method of funding has been suggested so as to enable the universities to enhance the quality of on-going programmes and to launch market oriented courses while making students pay for it. Currently, the education of students from higher income groups is heavily subsidized and this contributes to perpetuation of socio-economic disparities. In the approach suggested above, the beneficiaries would pay according to their ability or meet the educational expenses out of the interest-free loans while the education of poor sections of society would be suitably subsidized by the government. The financial dependence of universities on government would gradually decline and thereby minimize the government interference in the university autonomy. In this context, the measures for augmenting additional resources that have been suggested are upward revision of fee structure especially in professional courses; full recovery of cost of education from foreign students; mobilization of resources from industry by way of initiating relevant programmes for managerial and technical staff of industries and other commercial organizations, undertaking consultancy projects from industry; and revising users' charges for hostel, library and laboratory fee etc. Among the measures suggested for economy in expenditure are: to reduce the expenses on non-academic activities; to share facilities like national laboratories and libraries etc. with other local institutions; to increase the capacity utilization of infrastructure like classrooms, laboratories, libraries etc; to abolish the incredible examination system so as to avoid duplication of academic testing service; and to centralize the system of admission to various courses offered by colleges and universities on a regional basis so as to minimize the wasteful expenditure by reducing the duplication of activities relating to processing of applications. All these measures have significant potential to enhance the resource base and productivity of the system that is a must for accelerating the pace of economic and social development.

Tilak (1994) has explored the idea of external assistance by the bi-lateral and multilateral agencies in the field of education. The economic problems have forced more and more developing economies to increasingly resort to external borrowing for education. In the area of external assistance for education there are several agencies – bi-lateral and multi-lateral official agencies and private agencies. The policies and the nature and type of aid of the several agencies have varying impact on the recipient countries. One of the most important shifts in the priorities of the international aid organizations relates to the shift in emphasis from sound technical principles of lending of the 1960s and 1970s to emphasis on professional issues in areas like education in the 1980s. But education is a late entry into external aid mechanism. It is also observed by the author that between the bilateral and multilateral agencies, in general, the multi-lateral agencies are increasingly becoming prominent in case of education assistance, and among the multilateral agencies, the role of the World Bank has been found to be singularly important, contributing about 20 per cent of total external assistance for education during the 1980s. It is argued by the economists that the World Bank's realization that investment in human capital would not only be economic, but also that investment in physical capital without corresponding investments in human capital in the developing countries would not yield high sustainable returns, forced the World Bank to enter education.

The study adds that all aid agencies did not have a common set of priorities, nor have the priorities of a given organization remained the same over the years. Science and technology figured prominently in the policies of the several aid agencies in the first development decade. It was science and technology for many organizations like the British Council, USAID etc, while it was technical and vocational education for the World Bank, when it got interested in diversified secondary education. Until the early 1960's the World Bank had literally no role in funding education in developing countries. When it started its work in education, it first concentrated on higher education, later on secondary education and during the most recent years on primary education, when the attention of the international agencies shifted in favour of poverty alleviation. The added vigour of the campaign for "Education for All" in the recent past owes at least partly to the World Bank. The World Bank now lays more reliance on quality of education as against stress on quantitative expansion of the 1960's and 1970's. The research policies of the aid agencies have not contributed to building up of the developing countries. But it is also felt that much of the criticism of the World Bank is due to overlooking the fact that the World Bank is first and foremost a bank.

Oberoi (1995) gives some important solutions to the problems discussed by various committees and commissions. Several views are expressed in this paper, which give proper solutions needed for our present problems related with educational scenario. The various commissions, committees, policies and the institutions of higher education have missed the deeper relationship between the tradition and the reforms. The starting point for any reform is a detailed analysis of traditions and the proposed changes to be implemented after consensus among those who are responsible for implementation at institutional level. One very important suggestion is that Teachers Associations is very crucial in brining about any reform in higher education system. Such consultations and consensus should be prerequisite for policy change and when that happens it would necessitate a fresh look at the education and re-education of those characters that are to teach in higher education over and above the two points mentioned above. Character building activities at school and college level must be added on the agenda of the commissions, committees and policies for the 21st century. It is also pointed out that our higher education system has expanded at a very rapid rate to provide opportunities for social mobility to the people who were deprived of it for a long time. However, they admit that the large scale expansion has resulted in unemployment of graduates and deterioration in the quality of education; it has also resulted in the emergence of a dominant student body those who are interested only in acquiring a degree for a job or social status; learning and intellectual developments are not their motives.

Tilak (1995) has made an attempt to examine the arguments of the 'neo-liberal' economists and the economists believing in welfare state philosophy. Specifically, the paper looks at the several approaches of cost recovery in education of public expenditure that is financed through user payments, mainly the students being identified as users. The author has given several arguments in favour and against the cost recovery approach in relation to education. The author feels that the overall case against cost recovery is relatively stronger. In another section the author concentrates on a few methods of cost recovery, and critically examines some of the available empirical evidence from a cross section of countries on the relative effects of various methods. The author has discussed in detail the public good characteristic of education, which has valuable implications for financing and cost recovery in education. Important measures of cost recovery that have been discussed and/or are being experimented with in several developing and developed counties include (a) student fee; (b) student loans; and (c) ear marked taxes which include the (i) payroll tax (it is an education specific tax to be levied on those who use the educated manpower); (ii) Graduate tax (the graduates pay a proportion of his/her income for a part or whole of his/her working lives as a kind of repayments for the costs of his/her education); (iii) Educational cess (earmarked levy, payable by all members in a given region, and its revenues are to be used for a specific purpose, education in case of an education cess). The main limitation of the paper is that it does not discuss several important issues relating to overall financing of education. It foresees on some important measures of cost recovery only. As all cost recovery measures are also inherently inequitable, some advocates of cost recovery suggest the need for scholarships along with their proposals for cost recovery, to protect to some extent, the poor from with drawing from education. But the issue of scholarships has not been discussed in the paper.

In another work, **Tilak** (1995) has discussed the issue of funding of higher education in India and related issues. The work analyzes the two reports: (i) UGC report of the "Committee on Funding of institutions of Higher Education" and (ii) the AICTE report on "Mobilization of Additional Resources for Technical Education". These two reports contain several analogous arguments and suggestion on wider policy issues and specific procedural matters. These reports have been prepared after the new economic policies were introduced in the country. So they spell out, in the changed context the need for new strategies for funding higher education that has serious short, medium and long-term implications. There is also an urgent need for improving the mechanism for the allocation and for the UGC/Government grants to universities and institutions of higher education grants mechanism based on unit cost formulas are the minimum needed reforms in this direction and efforts should also be made to raise resources from non-governmental sources to supplement governmental resources but this should be done without effecting equity and efficiency in education. Tilak advocates that the state cannot abandon its responsibility of funding higher education and shift the ones to the market forces. There should be a modest and gradual increase in fees to cover about 20-25 per cent of the recurring costs of higher education along with introduction of a well designed scholarship and student loan programmes and resources could also be generated through voluntary donations and other contributions from corporate sector, through tax increase on the one side and incentives in use of these funds by the institutions in use of these funds by the institutions on the other side.

Mathew, E.T. (1996) elaborates the private financing system of education. Privatization of higher education essentially means increasing reliance on private sources of educational finance in place of ever-increasing government subsidies. Cost recovery becomes a major instrument of privatization of education. Higher education offers ample opportunities for participation by both private and public sectors. The inadequacies or rigidities arising from exclusive reliance on either sector or any one form of private initiative can and should be corrected by diversifying the mode of financing. Whether individual institutions of higher education are formally classified as public/private or not, the most sensible option under the prevailing conditions in India is not only to broaden the financial base of higher education, but also to restructure higher education in terms of courses and content in order to make it more relevant. Under no circumstances, however, the entire cost of providing higher education should be recovered from the immediate beneficiaries, that is, exactly what the self-financing colleges seek to accomplish. Instead, besides the students currently enrolled as many supporting agencies as possible such as alumni, industry, philanthropists, foundations, trusts and endowments should be involved in financing education. Several methods of cost recovery are given in this article as: (a) enhancement of tuition and other fees; (b) student loans; and (c) earmarked Taxes.

Dhesi (1998) has emphasized that education is an important investment in human capital. It builds the technical capabilities of a society. So there should be a proper developmental strategy and allocation of resources. Clearly defining societal objectives that would vary with the level of development and their corresponding reflection in intra-sector priorities is necessary to achieve optimum results. In the context of planned development, mass literacy, generation of skills of various types and levels were considered priority areas in education. However, development strategy adopted by India, with excessive emphasis on modern urban-based industry in a protected environment had an inbuilt bias for investment in higher education. The institutional structure as evolved in the context of a centralized development strategy adopted by India has created strong incentives for individuals to seek higher education and employment in the modern sector. Three complimentary places of data used to identify the priorities within the education system - resources intensity (measured by unit cost), coverage and the extent of govt. subsidization - suggest that there is a structural bias in favour of higher education. Subsidy also tends to increase with the level and very low cost recovery; private rates of return to education are higher than the social ones. Returns to professional higher education are higher than those to general education. In general, social costs increase much more rapidly than private costs with the level of education. Due to this gap between private and social costs, expected private returns increase more rapidly than private costs. So a rational individual should aspire to acquire as much education as possible with supply of education being highly responsive to social and political pressures, an inbuilt tendency sets in for expansion of higher education resulting in increased misallocation of resources in terms of social costs, but as supply of graduates outstrips the generation of job opportunities, educated unemployment increases. Initially, the educated joins the ranks of unemployed with a strong tendency for the education level among them to rise. The better educated among them tend to lower their aspirations and accept jobs and respond by raising the formal educational entry qualifications for jobs. Thus excess qualifications for jobs become formalized. Because of trade union pressure, wages get linked to the levels of education attainment of employees, and link between wage and productivity breaks down. The existing distortions in wage differentials get magnified, thus stimulating the demand for higher education even further. Those who for some reason are unable to continue their education suffer the most. Unless a proper functioning reward and cost structure promoting equity and efficiency in development and allocation of human capital is instituted, society has to go on bearing high social costs.

Therefore, from societal view point, it would be rational to give priority in public spending to basic education with relatively high social returns and to increase private share of costs with the level of education. The bias in public spending in favour of higher education has made the education system largely dysfunctional. Vast sections of the society have been deprived access to quality basic education; it also creates excess demand for higher levels of education.

Supply of education being highly responsive to political pressure, the bias in public spending has led to an unplanned expansion of higher education with declining standards. Some of the major reasons for this, unhealthy situation have been education system's over dependence on government finance and structural bias towards highly subsidized higher education constraining the total resource availability. The bias in public spending towards higher education coupled with unplanned expansion in response to political pressures has made the education system fiscally unsustainable. Therefore, the objective of policy should be to bring down the growth rate of higher education to a more realistic, fiscally sustainable level and to ensure equity and efficiency in public spending.

Punelekar (1998) has emphasized that all sectors of the Indian economy-industry, trade, finance - are opening up, and so also are social services sector, including education. This is a conscious and decisive shift in policy that the Indian state has chosen for restructuring India with the focus on competition and privatization, deregulation and decontrol. Like a few other sectors, education is a strategic sector of the Indian economy and society, substantive changes within which may have long-term consequences for its future growth and direction. The author says that it is needless to emphasize that one has to concentrate on emerging prospects and pitfalls of privatization in education, especially its impact on higher education and the quality of labour force that may be built up through formal education, skill up gradation outlets and training in science and technology. It adds that we have to keep in mind that in our efforts to create a trained manpower, we cannot gloss over some basic issues of equity and justice to which we have all committed ourselves through India's constitution and planned interventions in the social life of its citizens. But while shifting radically and in haste towards the privatization path, there is need for a fair and objective evaluation of what went wrong with the earlier education policy and programmes and their underlying normative message. Because of the limits on the resources which the govt., can spend on education, there is an urgent need to make available the resources from private hands. So in recent times, privatization of education is felt necessary.

Samal (1999) has analyzed the need for private financing in education. Author is of the view that education is an investment that contributes to individual and social development, so no single nation in the world with illiterate and uneducated people is developed and advanced. Growth of conventional inputs: physical capital, labour and land are an essential but not a sufficient condition for increasing national output. The other most important input is human capital, skilled manpower. From ancient times right up to the early stages of capitalist development education services were financed by private sources. In recent times, two conflicting phenomena have been observed: (i) decline of State resources; and (ii) expectation of increase in emolument. Because of resource constraints in the states, efforts are being made to mobilize private resources. Thus there is an increasing reliance on market forces. But reduction in state financial support results in sacrifice of quality, particularly in higher and technical education. The author has recommended various measures to recover the cost of higher education: (a) upward revision of tuition fee; (b) education loan; (c) graduate tax; (d) payroll tax; (e) brain-drain tax; (f) education cess; and (g) selection of teacher, students and quality of courses.

Utilizing the pooled data for 15 large Indian States over the period 1992-93 to 1997-98, **Roy, Kamaiah** *et al.* (2000) study the expenditure on education. Their study has found that though education is included in the Concurrent List, the major responsibility of providing educational facilities rests on the State governments. The proportion of revenue expenditure spent on education across the 15 large

States is of uneven nature. This uneven nature of expenditure might be attributed to the unequal level of development and presence of social pressure groups in these states. By utilizing the data for states this study employs a panel data models to estimate the normative (average) levels of expenditure on primary, secondary and higher education. The findings of the study reveal that the actual spending on educational services in low-income states is lower than their 'needs'. In other words, the higher (lower) the per capita expenditure on education, the higher (lower) is the emphasis the state lies upon provision of education. Because such a view may be misleading when there are significant cost variations in the provision of education services across the states, so to meaningfully assess the relative position of the states, it is felt necessary to ascertain the cost of providing a 'standardized' unit of educational service across the Indian states. So it was felt that estimating an all India average (normative) cost of providing a standardized unit of educational service might prove to be more meaningful. The present work proceeds from the supply (cost) side and attempts to estimate the normative expenditure levels with regard to expenditure on education for 15 large Indian states for the fiscal year 1997-98. On the basis of normative expenditures this paper proceeds further to make a comparative analysis of the normative and actual expenditure level's with the objective of classifying states on the basis of the relative emphasis laid on the provision of education. For a meaningful analysis, expenditure on education is categorized into three heads as primary, secondary and higher. The expenditure considered in this study relates to total revenue expenditure, which is the sum total of non-plan and plan revenue expenditures.

Shariff and Ghosh (2000) examine the different dimensions of the financial scenario of education in India and its states. Despite expert advocacy of an increase in the share of public expenditure on education in India's GNP, the share declined between 1990-91 and 1991-96 of this expenditure, elementary education accounts for less than half-against the two-thirds plus deemed necessary. At least in respect of elementary education it should be possible, given political will, to bridge the resource gap. The work concludes that: (a) the annual rate of growth of expenditure as a whole has been declining and this trend is more or less similar for all levels of education and the relative share of elementary education in the total education budget has declined over time in most states; and (b) the share of education in the budgets of most state governments has declined significantly. This decline is particularly conspicuous because structural adjustment and stabilization policies have accorded low priority to social sectors like education. This has had quantitative and qualitative impact on education; (c) State-wise figures reveal that per pupil expenditure on education, especially by the less developed states has also declined. It adds that the government will need to expand its role in contributing resources, especially in respect of elementary education to some of the poorer states.

Vedagiri (2000) analyzes the report of committee on plan projects that was constituted as a result of recommendations of the Taxation Inquiry Commission. This commission studied the entire structure of taxation in the country and suggested that there should be a setup for effectively evaluating the plan projects with a view to suggesting measures for economy and efficiency. The committee on plan projects was set up as a consequence towards the end of 1956. The main terms of reference of the committee were in locating the deficiencies in the planning and execution of projects and suggesting remedies for cost reduction specifically in construction projects in different sectors as agriculture, community development, transport, public works and buildings. There is considerable amount of construction activity for social services like education, health etc. The author is of the view that there is over-capitalization everywhere though its quantum may vary and to reduce it one has to know the fundamental principle of how capital formation takes place on these construction works. According to this study, the scope for cost reduction is more in early stages named pre-planning and planning stages. The pre-planning stage mainly devotes a stage where the requirements of the project are crystallized. The next stage of planning embraces architectural planning, structural planning and quantity surveying. Taking the examples of school buildings in Delhi, laboratories of schools, an out patient department of a hospital, hostels the author has stressed the need for cost reduction measures in every sector of the economy.

III

UNIT COST OF EDUCATION

Kamat (1967) has attempted to evolve a method of determining the current institutional cost per student per year in the colleges of Arts, Science and Commerce. The general principles and procedure have been outlined and applied to the expenditure data of two colleges in Poona and thus obtaining current institutional cost per student for undergraduate courses in Arts, Science and Commerce. It is found that the cost in running a commerce course is much lower and that in running a science course is much higher than the cost in running an Arts course. The cost of education is interpreted in two different ways: (a) student cost and (ii) institutional cost. Institutional cost, particularly the recurring part of the institutional cost, has been analyzed. The items of expenditure are also separated under two categories: (i) common or non-divisible expenditure and (ii) divisible expenditure on the purchase of equipment as books and journals for the library or apparatus for the laboratories is included in the non-recurring cost but in this study it comes under recurring cost. The work has analyzed the unit institutional cost in higher education, but no attempt has been made in this study to estimate the student cost or private cost. The work has taken into consideration the recurring expenditure only and has not covered the non-recurring component. In the estimation of current or recurring costs, no allowance has been made for depreciation on the capital investment.

Datt (1981) has observed that the pattern of financing higher education shows an elitist bias and as such, it is iniquitous. An effort should be made to make it rational from the point of view of equity and social justice. The University of Delhi imparts instruction via four different techniques. There are regular colleges and teaching departments of the university; secondly, the university, has evening colleges; thirdly the school of correspondence courses; fourthly, there is non-collegiate woman delegacy. Besides this the university permits students to appear as private candidates under the External Cell. The author has managed to procure data for fee and other income and expenditure from the budgets of the institutions. Sample under consideration consists of ten morning colleges, three evening colleges and the budgets of non-collegiate women delegacy and the school of correspondence courses. The data pertain to the year 1976-77. From the analysis of distribution of expenditure, it is obvious that in higher education, bulk of the expenditure, nearly 87-89 per cent is incurred on staff salaries and other teaching aids such as library audio-visual equipment, laboratory apparatus, overhead projectors, printed synopsis of lectures etc. do not receive much attention. There appears to be strong justification for cutting down the salary component of expenditure and substituting it with equipment of modern educational technology. Although, it is difficult to measure the efficiency because the educational product is multidimensional in nature, but still the author has defined efficiency in a very limited sense. The purpose of the institution is to make the student learn so as to succeed in the examination and secure a degree. Various studies have also pointed out that performance at the present examination is highly correlated with performance at the previous examination socio-economic background of students also plays an important part in the performance of the students. Besides this, the quality of teachers and the supporting services available at the institutional level also determine efficiency. Since regular college students are qualitatively better off students in terms of their performance at the previous examinations and they have better socio-economic backgrounds, the differences in pass percentage only reflect this initial qualitative difference in input. The institutional factor does not appear to be dominant. There is a need to: (a) economize expenditure in regular colleges and university departments without impairing efficiency; (b) to generate more internal resources by revising the fee structure; and (iii) to develop norms of staffing pattern and other supporting services to be provided in non-collegiate women delegacy, correspondence courses and evening colleges. There are two principal sources of funds: (i) income from fees and other sources and (ii) grants from UGC. Internal resources depend upon the level of fees charged. The fear of organized student union reaction has prevented universities and the UGC, to revise the fee structure. To generate more internal resources this fee structure needs to be revised.

The objective of **Goel's** Study (1985) is to know the private cost of post-graduate general education and as such the faculties of commerce, law and teacher education were excluded. The students undertaking post-graduate general education have been surveyed with the help of a well-structured questionnaire. The students are divided according to the nature of their residence, into various categories. The data relate to the academic session 1977-78 for post-graduate students enrolled at Gorakhpur University. The work has defined cost of higher education in detail in the beginning. The work analyses the underlying dynamics of cost of education.

The study by **Prakash and Bansal** (1985) had been undertaken with a view to get an idea about the unit cost of college education in Punjab and its variation among colleges of different types and sizes. The study of unit cost enables one to estimate the cost of operating the existing educational institutions from which one can have an idea about the degree of cost effectiveness or the efficiency with which the system operates in a given situation. This enables the policy makers, planners and the administrators to discover the gaps in the functioning of the educational institutions. It also reveals the determinants of the unit cost that may suggest alternative educational policies to be pursued in future. The study is based on the primary data collected from the office of Directorate of Public Instructions (DPI), (Colleges), Punjab. In this study, the unit cost has been measured only at a point of time. This limits the usefulness of the study. Various statistical techniques like fitting of regression equations, correlation and regression etc. have been used by the authors in analyzing the data obtained from the sample of 159 colleges studied. The study concludes that salary is the major component of total recurring cost in the college education.

Gupta (1986) has analyzed the income and expenditure of correspondence education for the state of Rajasthan. The study is based on the data from Institute of Correspondence Studies, University of Rajasthan, Jaipur. The broad conclusion of the study is that the income of the institute has come to stay, but the expenditure is rising, therefore if the income is to be matched with the expenses, attempt should be made to increase the income, and to increase the income, the work proposes many alternatives as: (a) the emolument charges from the students in these courses should be increased; (b) the per capita fee charged from the students should be increased; and (c) alternative sources of income such as grants from the organizations as UGC and State government should be sought.

Ramalingaswamy (1986) has discussed how the costs can be calculated in an institution, particularly in the medical institutions. The study has given techniques and principles of the calculation of costs and has drawn many conclusions. With regard to capital cost one thing that has become clear is that it is very high if one takes into account the initial costs with the price ranges and the prevailing value of the rupee at the time the college is constructed. The recurring institutional cost varied according to the assumptions made in imputing the hospital costs for educational purposes. The faculty scales of pay and the number of students admitted influenced the recurring expenditure involved in educating a medical graduate. College which had higher scales of pay for the faculty and which had admitted fewer students, showed higher cost per student. Since the time this data was collected, there has been an increase in prices in general and in the pay scales of the faculty in some colleges and in the stipends paid to the interns and house surgeons in all colleges. If the recurring costs were to be worked out now for the same colleges by using the same technique, there is bound to be an increase in these costs. As the technique itself is simple it is suggested that institutional costs be estimated at least once in two years.

Tilak (1987) has attempted a detailed analysis of costs of education in two educational clusters in Haryana. It presents estimates of the total and unit cost of education in two education clusters, Kherla and Punhana in Haryana's Gurgaon district and analyses them by levels, types of schools and by components. An exercise has been carried out to examine the determinants of costs as well. As previously mentioned, non-recurring costs constitute a negligible proportion of total costs of education and of the several components of recurring costs teacher's salaries and allowances constitute the bulk. In absolute terms a petty amount of less than a rupee is spent on items like books and journals and supporting material. First, the unit cost of education by components has been estimated for the two clusters separately and then an attempt is made to present an aggregate picture of the two. The work deals with school level of education. Education Commission (1966) had suggested long ago the adoption of the system of the 'school complex' or 'school cluster' which can be defined as a cluster of inter-linked primary, resources to start a new institution. As far as the changes in the unit costs over time, the total average unit cost of all levels and types of education taken together has increased in all middle, high schools and colleges located in the area. Non-recurring costs have been excluded in this study. Unit costs of education are on the whole higher in the two clusters than the estimates of costs corresponding to their blocks. The estimates are also found to be higher than those of the district as a whole. The different estimate have not been consistent with regard to which cluster incurs higher unit costs than the other. On the whole, the cost of primary level education in the Punhana cluster is higher than that in the Kherla cluster, and the opposite is the case with respect to secondary education. Thus the work concludes that the level of economic development of a region has not affected systematically the cost of education.

Further, the non-formal and adult education in the clusters are much cheaper than the costs of the same in the blocks of Sohna and Punhana, as well as in the district of Gurgaon, as a whole of course it is also cheaper than formal education. An important finding, having serious policy implications is that as far as the salary cost of the teachers per student is concerned, primary education is cheaper, if provided in the secondary or middle schools than in the primary, schools and the total, including teacher's salary and other, recurring costs of primary-level education is not substantially higher than that in the primary schools. In the Punhana cluster both teachers' costs and total cost of primary level education are less if provided in secondary schools, than in exclusively primary schools. Such schools help in reducing the dropouts and stagnation quite significantly. Thus such a system, besides reducing both normal and effective cost significantly by reducing dropouts, may also help in solving the quality of primary education on the one hand and in integrating primary education sector with the middle and secondary levels on the other. It is found that of the several possible factors that could be identified, the pupil-teacher ratio is the most dominant variable in determining the unit costs of education and hence it can be used for regulating costs of education, if necessary.

Panda and Padhi (1990) have analyzed the cost effectiveness in higher education, particularly the higher education in the state of Orissa with particular reference to commerce education. Higher education in science, humanities and commerce fulfils a variety of needs of our economy. At the same time these educated persons swell the supply in manpower market. So planners have started emphasizing on education that would create jobs rather than job seekers. The work has elaborated the importance of proper planning in commerce education. This study is based on some postulates: (a) Commerce education is costlier than science and humanities; (b) The faculty suffers from low capacity utilization; and (c) The faculty does not stimulate entrepreneurial attitudes. These postulations have been derived from the currently held opinion at planning and decision making stages of the state government and also the traditional belief of the society in Orissa. One post-graduate college (Khallikote College, Behrampur) has been selected for the study. It is situated at the nerve center of Commerce in the Southern region of Orissa. The right education imparted with minimum cost is referred to as cost effectiveness. In this study focus is on some proxy variables of cost effectiveness: (i) enrolment; (ii) capacity utilization;

(iii) student-teacher ratio; (iv) unit cost per student of teaching staff; (v) unit cost per lecture; (v) unit cost per student of non-teaching staff; (vi) faculty cost for infrastructure facilities; and (vii) entrepreneurial attitude of commerce graduates. Maximum utilization of enrolment capacity is found in the commerce faculty. It shows an increasing trend. It is due to the increase in demand for commerce studies. The capacity of the commerce faculty tends to be optimally utilized due to the introduction of more vocational and demand-oriented courses in the commerce faculty as typewriting, shorthand, book-keeping, salesmanship, insurance system etc. Further due to the prospects of employment and recruitment to managerial jobs (commerce courses leading to accounting, cost analysts, secretary ship, entrepreneurship, marketing management etc). Now-a-days these courses are very much alluring and in demand. The work has analyzed various facets of effectiveness of education.

Nair, P.V. Bhaskaran (1990) has emphasized the fact that the cost of education is one of the main areas of research in economics of education. It occupies an important place, as studies in most other fields in economics of education are dependent on cost measurement. Cost estimates enable one to know beforehand how much is to be spent by a student/ parent for completing a particular course. They also help the policy planners to assess the quantum of assistance required per student for a particular course and make decisions on the investments to be made on education. Though this study pertains to a single university, viz. the University of Calicut, it is applicable to other affiliating universities in India as the cost structure is more or less similar in all the universities. An attempt has been made to present an exhaustive account of the estimates of all costs, namely private cost, public cost and social cost during each year and the entire period of the post graduate course in Humanities and commerce and science separately. The post graduate courses conducted in the colleges affiliated to the University have not been considered in this investigation as they do not directly come under the university administration and the work involved is enormous. While reviewing some of the related literature, author finds that while some studies have estimated only institutional cost, some others have attempted to work out private cost and a few others private and social costs. The study is based on both primary and secondary data. An examination of the cost structure in the two faculties for postgraduate education shows that there is only nominal difference in the overall average total private expenditure per student in the two faculties, i.e., in the faculty of science and in the faculty of Humanities and commerce. However, there is considerable difference in the public cost and therefore in the social cost also in the two faculties. The cost of postgraduate education in science is more than in commerce and humanities points to the necessity of restricting admission to the science faculty according to the manpower requirements to be estimated and absorbing those who complete their course in science in the specialized field.

Sahoo (1990) conducted a study with the objective of finding out the private costs of post-graduate students of Arts and Commerce disciplines keeping in view the independent variables like nature of courses and residential background of students. Mean Average and Chi-square tests have been used for analysis of data. Around 90 per cent of student's expenditure is incurred as non-tuition cost and the remaining 10 per cent is spent for tuition cost. Commerce students' expenditures are significantly higher than those of their Arts counter parts with regard to boarding and lodging, traveling and miscellaneous heads. While there does not exist significant difference between day scholars and residential students with regard to tuition costs and expenditures on books and stationeries, total private costs of residential students are almost seven times higher than that of day scholars. High rate of private costs may not be taxing on middle and upper middle class parents. Certainly economically poor parents find it difficult to afford high rate of expenditure on higher education of their offspring. One major implication of the study relates to enhancement of the revenue through the tuition costs, on the ground that the students are in a position to afford. As most of the students belong to Himanchal Pradesh and Punjab, i.e., having above average and nearer to average position in the distribution of national level per capita income, university education with such expenditure may not be taxing to the upper middle class parents, but the questions have been raised about the study facilities for middle and poor class students. In such cases the university authority should concentrate on enhancement of financial support and residential facilities for backward section students.

Mathew (1991) held that the higher education offers ample opportunities for participation by both private and public sectors. The inadequacies or rigidities from exclusive reliance on either sector or any one form of private initiative can and should be corrected by diversifying the mode of financing. The most sensible option under the prevailing conditions in India is not only to broaden the financial base of higher education, but also to restructure higher education in terms of courses and content in order to make it more relevant. Under no circumstances however, the entire cost of providing higher education should be recovered from the immediate beneficiaries, which is exactly what the self-financing colleges seek to accomplish.

Sulochana (1991) has studied the finances of Osmania University. A variety of issues relating to paucity of funds and the existing mechanism for funding of higher education have been documented. It has been discovered in recent times that universities have been spending more on administrative and support activities than on academic activities and so has been the case with Osmania University.

The study reveals that the ratio of teaching and non-teaching staff has been declining in the university salaries on the non-teaching staff are more than the salaries of the teachers and the former has been rising at a faster rate than the later. Fees as a source of finance have been declining sharply while voluntary contributions in the form of donations and gifts have almost dwindled. It is also revealed that the cost of higher education over a period of time has increased manifold and the block grants from the state government and the development assistance from the University Grants Commission have been the major sources of finance in the Osmania University. It is also revealed that Osmania University gets lesser funds as compared to the newer universities of the state and that equitable system of funding for higher education, both at the national and the state level remains a far cry.

The main focus in the article by **Varghesc** (1991) is on the trends in changing management concerns in higher education and problems associated with introducing changes. The changing concerns in management of higher education is grouped into four phases: (i) management of expansion characterized by expansive institutionalization and diversification of structures of higher education; (ii) management of stabilization when growth in student enrolment and budgets for higher education slowed down and increased emphasis was placed on planning and budgetary controls; (iii) management of decline denoting a period of declining share of resources and student enrolment coinciding with the demand for increased accountability and institutional performance of institutions of higher education; (iv) management of adjustments referring to a period of severe budgetary cuts to the universities wherein they have to readjust their programmes and staff. It is emphasized in this paper that planning and monitoring are necessary conditions for successful implementation of any change in any university. In almost all the cases innate conservatism and resistance to change from within are found to be the major hurdles in implementing changes in the universities.

Jee-Peng and Alain Mingat (1992) in the study provide an overview of sectoral development, with an emphasis on cost and finance issues. This focus was chosen because education outcomes depend critically on resource allocation and allocation in turn is influenced by policy choices affecting costs and finance. The study had three main aims: to document current patterns of costs, finance and out comes in individual Asian countries; to explore linkages between sectoral performance and policy choices; and to identify potential policy options to promote efficient and equitable sectoral development. The study rests on a rich database compiled from valued sources. First section of the work presents the data set; next section describes the unit of costs of colleges and universities by type and location of college and by university faculty. It also examines the distribution of expenditure by budgetary category and the size and distribution of teaching and non-teaching staff. Third section investigates economies of scale across institutions and identifies institutional characteristics (e.g. student – faculty ratios, student-non-faculty ratios etc.) that explain variation in costs across institutions. Fourth section presents college student examination pass rates and identifies factors that explain variation in achievement across institutions. Last section describes patterns of revenues and cost recovery and the grant allocation process. The whole analysis supports the conclusion that higher education sector as it currently exists in Pakistan is undefended. University deficits increase annually and many colleges resemble primary schools with high student teacher ratios, low per student expenditure and trivial sums spent on operational expenses and instructional materials. This low resource base has had a negative impact on the quality of education resulting in failure for the majority of college students. Cost recovery in colleges and universities is low.

Although there is considerable potential to raise student fees, institutions depend heavily on government funding.

Sharma (1992), in his work has made an in-depth inquiry into the financial practices in Indian universities. The main objective of the study being a detailed analysis and critical evaluation of existing practices of financial management and control, it aims at highlighting the strengths and weaknesses of the system. It, thus explores the possibilities of improvement in the working and management of universities. Analysis is based on primary data collected through three distinct sets of questionnaires and it represents nearly one fifth of the total universities in the country. Besides, university-wise and state-wise secondary data on the sources of finance and expenditure pattern for the years 1982 to 1985 have been used. The work analyses the composition of recurring and non-recurring expenditure in the selected universities as well as in States of the country, and, on the other hand, also probes into the occurrence of deficit in some of the universities with a view to assess its impact on the working and performance of the system as a whole. However, it suffers from a few limitations as well. One of its major handicaps arises on account of the fact that most of the recommendations for improvement in the system, as made by the author, are based on his personal opinion and convictions alone. None of the recommendations are sustainable by scientific evidences and thus they remain untenable to a scientific mind.

Azad (1995) has discussed the problem of resource mobilization and has given some alternative strategies to finance higher education. The resource crunch for higher education is not a temporary phenomenon. The ushering in for the era of liberalization, decontrol and encouragement to private sector under the new economic policy does not necessarily mean that privatization of higher education is the only panacea for improving the economies of institutions of higher education. While we should welcome the participation of private bodies in the financing and administration of institutions of higher education, the government cannot and should not abdicate its responsibility of financing higher education. Higher education is too important an enterprise to be left to the whims of private organizations. There is also a need for mobilizing alternative sources of finances for higher education. In this connection, a package programme has been suggested that includes raising resources through enhancement of fees, laying emphasis on loans rather than grants and harnessing private and industrial resources. The other component of the programme is plugging the leakages that occur because of the large-scale wastage of resources in the form of failures in examinations, the under utilization of academic and physical infrastructure etc. It has also been suggested that an Educational Development Bank may be set up for providing soft loans to university institutions and administering a more comprehensive scheme of loan scholarships. Lastly the educational institutions, particularly at the higher education stage should be made accountable to public. There should be a system of continuously monitoring their performance and the non-viable institutions should be encouraged to close down. The autonomy and accountability of institutions should co-exist rather than being mutually exclusive.

Desai (1995) has stressed the need for development of higher education and make the universities more viable. The road to the development of a nation is through the education system and if we compromise on education at any level, we will jeopardize the socio-economic development of the country. There is no denying the fact that tremendous increase in scientific and technical manpower has provided. Educational systems of developing countries have been experiencing many stresses and strains. The major problems and issues are: (a) unplanned expansion having no proper link with market demand; (b) phenomenal growth with uneven distribution social, geographical and rural-urban; (c) deterioration in academic standards and management; and (d) inadequacy, inefficiency and ineffectiveness in the higher education finance. Among the policies suggested to mobilize additional resources for higher educational resources for higher education, the following have been mentioned: (a) increasing student fees and transferring more financial responsibility to direct beneficiaries; (b) expansion of commercial activities by universities and colleges; (c) cooperative programmes between higher education institutions and government agencies, industry and commerce; (d) better utilization of university and college land and other resources to generate income; (e) efforts to attract gifts and set up endowment funds; (f) attracting increased funds from overseas; and (vii) establishment and expansion of a private higher education sector. A wide range of policy measures are suggested to achieve greater cost-efficiency which include: (a) better utilization of buildings and equipment; (b) rationalization of teaching programme and institutions; (c) extension in the use of distance education and expansion of open universities; (d) use of more teacher efficient teaching methods (e) improvement in student progression and graduation rates; (f) improved planning and use of clear criteria and controls for the establishment of new institutions; (g) increased autonomy to individual institutions; (h) application of new or improved management methods; and (i) improved training of administrators and managers.

Ghuman (1995) has compared the private costs in both the systems: (i) the distance education and (ii) conventional education in India. As per the study, conventional education is very costly as compared to the distance education. The most expensive head in conventional education is that of board and lodging. It is a very interesting finding that if we deduct the cost of board and lodging from the total unit private cost of resident scholars; it comes out to be very near to the unit private cost of unemployed outstation distant learners. But it is still higher than the unit private cost of day scholars and local distant learners and distant learners combined. This combined with the social or public cost, which is substantially higher in conventional education as compared to distance education, makes conventional education all the more expensive. Keeping in view the lesser public private costs of distance education, the financial constraint of the Indian economy, the ever-rising demand for higher education and the rapidly growing population, distance education would be the most suitable system of education. It has, in fact, become a historical necessity. The future of Indian education lies in distance education. So it should be improved and strengthened in the country.

Dutt, Ruddar (1995) discusses about the problems related with the calculation of unit cost of education. Because of the non-availability of reliable and comprehensive data of assets and liabilities, the work excluded the estimation of capital cost of education. So the work discusses only the current cost of education which is a point estimate pertaining to the year 1965-66, although it suffers from all the related problems. The study covers the 'arts colleges' of Haryana only, which are the colleges that provide higher education, i.e., education after matriculation in arts, science and commerce. Out of 38 colleges, only 28 have been included because the consistent data for only 28 colleges were available with the U.G.C. Out of the sample of 28 colleges, 24 are maintained by privately aided governing bodies and 4 are being run by the state government. Out of 24 private colleges, 7 colleges impart instruction to girls only. Similarly out of 4 state colleges, one is a women college. On the basis of emoluments, it has been found that 58.5 to 64.4 per cent of the recurring cost is contributed by emoluments of teaching and non-teaching staff only. As per the study, the factors upon which unit cost of education depends are conditioned by the attitude of those authorities that are directly or indirectly concerned with the running of these institutions. Out of so many factors affecting unit cost, 'Age of the College' is one because a college requires a few years to mature depending upon the type of courses started and the time-period of each course. Cost of education is also affected by enrolment. Average pay of a teacher that is teacher costs are a major component of unit costs. Another factor is ratio of non-teacher to total cost, i.e., as the enrolment improves and as the age of college advances there is a need of more administrative staff. Besides this, library and reading room facilities, games and sports, other co-curricular activities are enlarged to meet the demands of the enlarged population of students. Different demerits of cost have been explained with the help of regression and correlation technique. Although this study is a comprehensive explanation of unit cost, but because of the non-availability of time-series data, the scope and coverage is too narrow.

The study by **Salim** (1995) attempts to analyze the extent of subsidization of higher education by the institution/ government and whether the present system of subsidization of higher education is appropriate in view of the socio-economic and the paying capacity of the parents of the students? In order to analyze the trend of government subsidization, institutional costs (recurring and non-recurring) and the fee receipts of the college for the period 1976-90 have been considered. In addition primary data based on an intensive field survey of two engineering colleges and two Arts and Science Colleges of Kerala has also been used. The study shows that the contribution of fees in the institutional cost is only marginal and declining. Now significant fall is noticed in the per-pupil cost, thus perpetuating the cost-fee disparity. The overwhelming burden of financing higher education has fallen on the govt., which is gradually taking up the role that fees had played earlier. The system of higher education has turned into an almost entirely government financed proposition. Surprisingly, subsidization is higher for technical education that generates larger private benefits than does general education. Further, as experienced by the state of Kerala in past decades, a good number of these students go abroad after completing their studies, thus transferring in the process, the benefits of the costly investment made on their education to other countries. All these facts cause concern over the present subsidization policy. It has been found that higher education, particularly professional education, is mostly appropriated by the students belonging to the middle and upper income groups and those from the high level occupation groups and forward communities. The benefits of the liberal government subsidy thus go mainly to these privileged sections. Large-scale govt. expenditure on higher education is treated as a measure of bringing about equality of opportunity and improved income distribution. The present system of subsidization has not yielded the desired results. It has only aggravated the inequalities by its present financing and subsidy policy in higher education.

The students belonging to the better-off sections spend significantly larger amounts on incidental (mostly non-essential) items of expenditure than those from the low-income group. All these pieces of evidence point to the inappropriateness of the existing system of subsidization of higher education. The work also indicates the potential of the better-off sections of society to share a larger part of the institutional cost. They also lay bare the fact that the poor are not at all in a position to do so. It all suggests the introduction of a discriminatory system of fees with a discriminatory system of incentives. Under such a system high income groups that at present get higher education almost free of cost would be priced appropriately based on their capacity to pay while the low-income groups would be totally or partially exempted through a package of freeships/scholarships or loans.

In another study, **Salim** (1996) deals with issue of calculating institutional cost of Higher education particularly in case of the state of Kerala. As higher education in India has witnessed phenomenal growth during the period since independence, Kerala has also shown spectacular growth of its higher education during this period. The growth has led to an ever-growing resource drain from the public exchequer and private funds. The State government finds it impossible to divert more of its revenue resources for education, particularly higher education. The experience of Kerala shows that rational calculations have not played a decisive role in the allocation of funds for education. In order to bring about the required changes in the government's policy of expenditure on higher education, it is essential, as a first step, to gain insights into its cost structure. It is against this background, an attempt has been made to study the institutional cost of higher education in Kerala. In this study, estimation of institutional cost is central to the understanding of economic value of higher education. The estimates of costs made on the basis of a sample survey of colleges in Kerala. The work holds that it is much more expensive for institutions/government to create and maintain a seat of engineering education than do the same in general education. Among the components of recurring cost, teaching cost occupies a predominant proportion. Expenditure on library and games and sports constitutes a negligible proportion of the cost. In case of capital cost, buildings constitute a significant part of the institutional cost. Further the burden of the institution for maintaining a post-graduate student is much higher than that for a degree student. Finally, only a very small part of the institutional cost is covered by fee paid by students; and a major part of the remaining amount is liberally subsidized by the government. It is paradoxical that the extent of this subsidization is about four times higher for engineering education, which generates prospects of larger private benefits later for the user for outweighing the social benefits, than that of general education. The work adds that it is high time to revise the existing system of subsidization by types of higher education so as to reduce the overwhelming cost-fee disparity. In the present study, an attempt is made to estimate the institutional cost (recurring and non-recurring) per student by types and levels of higher education. But no attempt has been made in this study to estimate private costs and social costs of education.

IV

CONCLUSION

Review of the studies is indicative of the fact that the studies done so far are aggregative in nature and if desegregation is achieved, the coverage too small. In this context, a detailed disaggregate study of the college education is need of the time. The work in hand is an attempt in this direction.

Cost of Education

Conceptual and Empirical Issues

The main thrust of economic analysis of cost of education is to evaluate and guide the resource allocation decisions and utilization patterns. As already said, the main objectives of the study is to analyze unit cost, cost recovery and explore the cost saving operations for an effective educational planning and administration in college education in Punjab. In this context, following chapter deals with methodological issues related to cost of education. The chapter is divided into three sections: section one conceptualizes the cost and its components; next section describes the database of the study; and the last section briefly gives the tools used.

In typical sense, cost refers to all those expenditures which an entrepreneur/enterprise made in order to produce goods and services and to stay in the market. But a distinction has generally been made between cost and expenditure. All the spending made by any unit on supplying a particular service may not be the actual cost of that service because it may involve some amount of wasteful expenditure also. Therefore, cost as an economic category, encompasses all these unavoidable expenditures which are needed in order to perform an economic activity of a specified level and of a specified quality. Expenditure can be expressed only in monetary units, while cost can be expressed both in monetary and real or physical terms. In this context, the work basically deals with analysis of recurring cost and in a passing reference it has commented on non-recurring expenditure also but that does not deal at all with the basic logic of the dissertation.

I

CONCEPTUALIZATION OF COST AND ITS COMPONENTS

The economic conception of costs is much wider and goes beyond an accounting exercise. From the accounting sense, cost includes all those explicit costs like payments and charges expended by an enterprise to outside suppliers of various productive factors in order to get supply of specified amount of goods and services. These are in fact direct costs to a concern which it takes into account while making business decisions. However, economic cost of production besides accounting costs also involves opportunity costs and environmental costs. These are collectively being described as social costs associated with an economic activity.

Cost of education consists of two components: (a) Opportunity cost; and (b) Social cost. Social cost can be further sub-divided into: (i) Student cost (private cost); and (ii) Institutional cost. Private cost (student cost) of education is incurred by students or by their parents. Private cost can further be sub-divided into two components: (i) direct private cost; and (ii) indirect private cost of education. Direct private cost includes expenditure incurred by students or their parents on items such as fees, books, stationary, etc., whereas indirect cost of education (opportunity cost) refers mainly to earnings foregone by the students. Other expenses which become sort of a must for educated persons;

as expenses on newspapers and periodicals, expenses on more trendy and fashionable dresses and more frequent expenses on movies etc. may also be included in indirect cost of education. Information relating to private cost could be had only by means of sample survey because secondary data are generally not available. But there are certain conceptual and methodological problems relating to the measurement and relevance of earnings foregone. But this concept of 'Earnings foregone' as an item of indirect cost would be relevant in case of those students only who can participate in productive activities. Students in the age group of up to 18 years generally do not participate in economic activities. Earnings foregone cannot be treated uniformly for all students who come from different cultural and socio-economic backgrounds even though they may belong to those age-groups, persons from which may partake in economic activities. In countries such as India, people belonging to lower socio-economic classes do not send their children to educational institutions because they cannot afford to lose the incomes that their children earn. On the other hand, people belonging to higher socio-economic groups/classes do not expect their children to contribute to the income of the families till they attain a certain age. Then in economies where the incidence of unemployment, particularly among the educated, is very high, choice before students is not between education and employment. The choice is rather between unemployment with less education and unemployment with more education.

For an estimation of earnings foregone, there is a need to carry out an in depth study of wage and employment structure of the educated manpower. But in a country like India which is a developing country, data regarding these aspects are highly scanty.

These difficulties compelled us to confine our attention to the study of institutional cost. Institutional cost refers to that expenditure which is incurred by an institution for the production of education. We will have a monetary measurement of the real resources used by the educational institutions.

Another major difficulty arises in the measurement of non-recurring cost incurred by educational institutions is that these costs are incurred once for ever, but the prices of items of non-recurring cost change overtime. Then there is a problem whether the cost should be evaluated in prices at which items have purchased or at current prices. Utility of such items is not exhausted immediately after the item has been used once. They rather have a long life span and the life span of different items differs a good deal. In order to distribute such expenses over a long period of time, one should at least have an approximate estimate of the working life of the items of fixed cost. It further involves conceptual and empirical problems.

In our study we are measuring recurring cost part of educational cost only, at a point of time, though this limits the usefulness of the study. The main thrust area of our study is to examine unit cost of the college education in Punjab and its variations among colleges of different locations (urban, semi-urban and rural), ownerships (government, private aided and unaided colleges) and sizes (big, medium, or small).

Opportunity cost, a concept used in economics, consists of the loss of income that a student would have earned, had he gone in for employment instead of pursuing education. The earning potential of persons with different educational attainments being different, this cost will vary at different levels of education. In full employment economies it may not be very difficult to estimate this cost but in the context of the present Indian economy which is afflicted with a lot of unemployment and a great deal of under-employment, it is problematical whether this cost can at all be estimated with any reasonable degree of reliability.

Student cost consists of four parts (a) tuition and other fees; (b) cost of books, equipment and stationary; (c) cost of maintenance (boarding and lodging); (d) other sundry expenses. Fee cost consists of the tuition fee, laboratory fee, examination fee, admission fee, and other fees and charges that a student has to pay to the college and to other educational authorities concerned. Since this payment on the part of the student becomes the income of the institution, which is again spent as part of the institutional cost, it has to be omitted from one place while calculating the overall unit cost to avoid double counting.

As regards maintenance, the students can be divided into two categories: (a) hostellers and (b) day-scholars. The day-scholars can be further divided into two parts (i) those that stay with their parents and (ii) those that make their own arrangement outside the hostel. The cost of maintenance for all these categories will be different. For hostellers, it is easy to arrive at a correct estimate of cost, but it is not so easy in the case of day-scholars of either description. Other sundry expenses include clothing, pocket-money, entertainment and other miscellaneous expenses. The cost of these items would vary considerably according to individual tastes and habits and the economic status of the student or his parents.

Institutional Cost

Institutional cost can be divided into two parts: (i) non-recurring and (ii) recurring. The non-recurring cost can be further sub-divided as (a) capital cost and (b) equipment cost. Similarly recurring cost can also be divided into (a) non-divisible recurring cost; and (b) divisible recurring cost. Non recurring cost is the cost on buildings, library, equipment, furniture and others, while the recurring cost is the cost on salary to teaching staff, salaries and wages to non-teaching staff, chemicals and other consumable store, scholarships and stipends, etc., games and sports, hostel, maintenance of buildings, maintenance of equipment, library and others.

Building

Investment in buildings happens to be the largest single item of fixed cost. In fact in developing countries like India, building happens to be the single item of fixed cost. In fact in developing countries such as India, building happens to be the single largest factor constraining the expansion of educational institutions. But once a building has been constructed, its services become available for a very long period of time, whenever enrollment increases new buildings are not required to be constructed. Marginal adjustments by means of reallocation of space, partitioning of rooms, or substantial adjustments by means of multiple shifts can always be made. Obviously expenditure on the construction of the buildings is an item of fixed capital. However, we have distinguished between two types of expenditure on building, expenditure on the construction of new buildings or the extension of the old ones and the expenditure incurred on the routine and repairs of the existing buildings The second type of expenditure has been classified as recurring, for example expenses on repairs, white-washing, etc. are required to be incurred practically each year.

Library

It constitutes an essential part of an educational institution and every year each institution incurs substantial expenditure on books, journals, newspapers and periodicals. Once a book/journal have been purchased it becomes a part of the stock of books/ journals in the library which can be used again and again by several generations of teachers and students. From this point of view expenditure on these items may be treated as a part of fixed cost. However, if a new section of the same class is started or seats are increased in the existing section, the number of copies of the same book required will also increase. Similarly, to keep up with the advancement in knowledge, new titles are needed, which implies that with an increase in the number of students enrolled/or with an increase in the amount of knowledge produced, expenditure on books and journals is required to be incurred time and again. Hence, the expenditure may also be treated as expenditure on working capital. Besides this recurring expenditure on the binding of the books and journals, insecticides to protect these from white ants, racks, cupboards, etc is incurred each year. Therefore, this expenditure has also been divided into two categories: recurring and non-recurring. Recurring expenditure on library includes expenditure on binding, insecticides, newspapers, magazines of general interest, stationery for library, maintenance of the materials and such other sundry expenses.

Equipment

An educational institution requires equipment of various kinds. The common variety of these equipments are computers; painters; scanners; type-writers, duplicating machines, tools, instruments, and other equipment for the laboratories of science departments, electric fans, bulbs, etc. Once equipment has been installed it has its own life span and the number of these items is not required to be increased every time when there is an increase in enrolment. Even when additional equipment becomes necessary as a result of increase in the number of students enrolled, the increase is seldom proportional as investment in fixed capital. But expenditure on routine maintenance and repairs of this equipment is needed periodically and hence this component is treated as a part of recurring expenditure.

Games and Sports

Material for sports and games could be divided in two categories (i) those items which have a comparatively stable life such as nets, poles, tennis tables, and (ii) those items which have to be replaced at yearly or less than yearly intervals, such as shuttle cocks, balls, hockey sticks, players' uniform, bats and the like. Similarly, expenses have to be incurred each year on the transport, boarding and lodging of the college teams which participate in various tournaments. We have classified expenditure on the second group of items as recurring expenditure. However, expenditure on the second type of items constitutes the major proportion of total expenditure on games and sports.

Furniture

It is also an essential input of the educational industry such as equipment, furniture has also got a specified life and hence its services are utilized over a period of time. We have, therefore, classified it under the head of non-recurring expenditure. However, a certain amount of expenditure is incurred on the repairs and maintenance of furniture every year. Expenses on polishing, replacement of cane and other repairs fall under this category and we have treated this as recurring expenditure.

Salaries and Allowances

Each educational institution has to employ teaching as well as non-teaching staff, who have to be paid their wages and salaries. Teachers are the most important input in the educational process. Without them one cannot think of an educational institution at all. But the number of teachers employed in an institution is mainly a function of students enrolled. However, their numbers is also affected by such factors as the number of sections of a class, number of subjects taught, optional papers allowed to be offered and the teacher student ratio prescribed by the educational authority. However, the number of teachers is not strictly proportional to the number of students enrolled, even though the relationship between the two variables happens to be very strong. As the salaries of the teachers have to be paid every month, this constitutes an item of recurring expenditure.

Non-academic staff constitutes an auxiliary input of the educational production process; and the number of employees in the education sector is not greatly affected by the enrollment size. It rather depends upon the volume of the work which to some extent of course, depends upon enrollment. But there is no prescribed non-teaching staff-student ratio to be adhered to. Besides this non-teaching staff has not to grow in the same proportion which the enrollment increases. There wages and salaries to be paid regularly, hence like teachers' salary, wages and salaries of non-teaching staff are also treated as an item of recurring expenditure.

Chemicals and Consumables

For conducting scientific experiments in the laboratories, certain commodities like chemicals are needed time and again. Quantum of such items depends upon the number of students who have to conduct the experiments and the number of times a given expenditure is to be conducted by each student. Expenditure on such items has also been treated as recurring expenditure. Similarly, consumable stores like chalk, sticks, stationery have also been treated as falling in the category of recurring expenditure.

Scholarships and Stipends

The Government of India set before itself the task of establishing socialistic pattern of society which requires reduction of economic inequalities. Equalization of opportunity constitutes one of the most effective measure of reducing the economic inequalities and education is a powerful tool of equalizing the opportunities. Therefore the educational authorities have been striving hard to enable the meritorious but poor students and students from the weaker sections of the society to have an access to higher education. For this purpose number of scholarships, stipends and other concessions have been offered. Therefore, most of the educational institutions incur such expenditure which is recurring in nature.

Hostel

Most of the institutions of higher education are required to maintain hostel for the benefit of the non-resident students. As this is an expenditure incurred for the benefit of boarders, great proportion of this expenditure, particularly the recurring one, is recovered from the boarders in the form of room rent, water and electricity charges, amalgamated fund, messing charges, etc. Therefore this may not be an institutional expenditure, but more often than not, such expenses are subsidized by the institutions to a great extent. Other expenditures on the upkeep and maintenance including wages and salaries of the hostel staff, furniture, electrical fittings, repair and maintenance of buildings, recreational facilities. But because of the applicability of this expenditure to the boarders alone, we have not examined it as a separate category.

II

DATABASE OF THE STUDY

The study has used both the primary and secondary data. For secondary data, various published and unpublished reports have been used. Using a well structured questionnaire through personal interview method, primary data has been collected from ninety colleges of Punjab.

Sample of the Study

For economic analysis of cost, universe of the study is composed of 206 colleges of Punjab. There are 6,200 total numbers of teaching posts in college education sector in Punjab. Out of this, 2,154 posts are with the Government Colleges. For drawing a sample, stratified random sampling technique has been be used. The sample size of the study is more than 40 per cent of the universe. For drawing the sample, the universe has been divided into three strata: government colleges, government aided private colleges; and unaided colleges. Out of the universe, sample drawn is

Table 3.1

Breakup of the Sample

	Urban				Semi-urban				Rural				Grand Total
	Large	Medium	Small	Total	Large	Medium	Small	Total	Large	Medium	Small	Total	
Government	11	02	01	14	0	02	0	02	0	04	06	10	26
Aided	08	11	03	22	01	09	01	10	03	04	03	10	42
Unaided	0	05	02	07	0	01	04	05	0	06	04	04	22
Total	19	18	06	43	01	12	04	17	03	14	13	30	90

composed of 26 government colleges, 42 private aided colleges and 22 unaided colleges. Thus the total sample size is of 90 colleges (Table 3.1). Using a well-structured questionnaire, through personal interview method, primary data has been collected.

According to strength, we have categorized all the colleges into three broad categories: large colleges; medium colleges; and small colleges. Top 25 per cent in terms of strength have been termed as large sized colleges and the lower 25 per cent have been termed as small sized colleges. Rest of the middle 50 per cent are the medium sized colleges. In this way there are twenty three colleges in the first category, 44 in the second category and 23 colleges in the third category.

Location-wise we classified the colleges into three categories: urban; semi-urban; rural. In the first category, we have 43 colleges. In the second category, we have 17 colleges and in the third category, we have 30 colleges.

III

ANALYTICAL TOOLS

From the raw data obtained, the cost components and various cost related coefficients have been arrived at by using the above methodology. Basically the work uses the tabular technique of analysis. Wherever needed appropriate statistical tools like arithmetic mean, coefficient of variation, correlation and analysis of variance have also been used.

Structure of Higher Education

The on-going phase of privatization and liberalization, has given way to indifference and skepticism about education system in general and the higher education in particular. Resources are often in short supply. There is an urgent need to maximize the efficiency of inputs in the education sector and thereby eliminate the wastage of precious resources. Education sector is faced with the challenge of raising the effectiveness of utilization of available resources. The current decade U-turn in the economic policy changes has left, almost all the sectors open to hard realities of the market. Subsidized for decades together and nurtured in a planned economy and public sector kind of environment, like other sectors, education sector had never been prepared for a market-oriented approach. By plain economic logic, a market guided system requires a maximization of revenue and minimization of the cost. It is in this context that the economic analysis of cost and the cost recovery in college education is the need of the hour. This chapter analyses the structure of higher education in Punjab.

I

EDUCATION AND DEVELOPMENT

For the sustainable development of any nation, higher education is a major instrument for change. It has the important task of preparing leaders for different walks of life in social, political, cultural, scientific and technological arena. Higher education is both consumption good and an investment input. It is always associated with better employment, higher level of income and better status in society. The returns of higher education are not only of private nature, but also more significantly, there are social and national returns to higher education and its benefits are widespread and far reaching.

Education commands pivotal place in socio-economic development. The practitioners of development economics recognize it as the largest single contributor to economic growth. The spread of education both in the quantitative and qualitative spectrum entails tremendous growth potential by providing big push to the human capabilities. Human resource development is not only the crucial input but is also simultaneously the end product of all the development endeavour of a nation. The development literature abounds with the studies which rigorously establish that the countries with high rate of human capital formation have observed higher rate of overall growth. However the developing countries never accorded top priority to education sector while formulating their national developmental priorities.

The modern growth theory establishes a strong positive correlation between the education and economic growth. The countries which invested heavily in education realized higher growth rates than those which neglected the education (Solow, 1962, Psachropoulous, 1988 and Heggade, 1992). The inter-connections between the education sector and non-education sectors are very deep and they affect each other multi-dimensionally. The present advanced countries have been continuously according top priority to education by investing heavily in this sector. In all these countries, education up to a certain level is the complete responsibility of the state. Since mid 1980s, new theories of economic growth have emphasized the role of human capital as the key to economic growth and development. It is higher education that enriches the quality of manpower. This has been borne out from a recent study of 190 countries by the World Bank. The study revealed that while physical capital and natural wealth respectively accounted for 16 and 20 per cent of the total wealth of the country, the human capital is estimated to account for the remaining 64 per cent of the wealth. The proportion of human capital is close to 80 per cent in the advanced countries like Germany, Japan and Switzerland. On the other side, in sub-Saharan Africa, where human resources are very poorly developed, the proportion is very low and that almost half of the national wealth is still in the form of natural resources. Thus human capital is the product of higher education.

II

INDIAN EDUCATION SYSTEM

India's distinctiveness rests on great foundations, which were built by its ancient sages who relentlessly sought after the highest integral knowledge and perfection; as a result her culture has been sustained, even through periods of decline, with surprising continuity since remote antiquity. Education is a liberating as well as an evolutionary force, which enables the individual to rise from mere materiality to superior planes of intellectual and spiritual consciousness. Education is a dialogue between the past, present and future so that the coming generations receive the accumulated lessons of the heritage and carry it forward.

Independent India inherited a higher education system with strong colonial legacies. The planners of India were therefore faced with the immediate challenge of bringing about a basic transformation in its educational system to fulfil the developmental needs of the country. The education planners had recognized the bi-directional linkages between education and development. The need for a literate workforce was considered to be as essential in this context as the education and training of an adequate pool of highly skilled manpower. Considerable emphasis was also given to higher education to strengthen the educational system as a whole, and particularly to scientific and technological components therein, so as to meet the requirements of high-level capabilities in the realm of knowledge as well as skills. To achieve these objectives, the University Grants Commission (UGC) was set up as an apex national organization concerned with the establishment and maintenance of standards in higher education. The UGC acts as a vital link between the policy-making bodies of the government and institutions of higher education. (Raza, 1991, pp. 32-33).

Despite serious handicaps of means and resources, the country has built up during the last fifty years a very large system of education and has created a vast body of men and women equipped with a high order of scientific and technological capabilities, robust humanist and philosophical thought and creativity. Prior to independence the growth of institutions of higher education in India was very slow and diversification in areas of studies was very limited. After independence, the number of institutions has increased significantly. There are today 214 universities and equivalent institutions including 116 general universities, 12 science and technology universities, seven open universities, 33 agricultural universities, five women's universities, 11 language universities, and 11 medical universities. Besides, there are universities focusing on journalism, law, fine arts, social work, planning and architecture and other specialized universities. But, in spite of vast efforts over the past fifty years, it is only now that the country is slowly emerging out of the fetters of old ideas and rigid structures, built during the colonial rule. There is at present a demand for radical changes which have the potential to actualize a national system of education that was visualized during the freedom struggle.

Under the Constitutional scheme, "education" is in the concurrent list and the Union Government and the States exercise joint responsibilities. As a result, while the role and responsibilities of the States in regard to education remains unaltered, the Union Government accepts a larger responsibility to reinforce the national and integrated character of education, to maintain quality and standards, to study and monitor the educational requirements of the country as a whole in regard to manpower for development, to cater to the needs of research and advanced study, to look after international aspects of education, culture and human resource development, and in general, to promote excellence at the tertiary level of the educational pyramid throughout the country.

Higher education is a basic investment necessary to improve the overall quality of life. For instance, with nearly half of the State's budget being earmarked for education and health related activities, Kerala has attained a Physical Quality of Life Index (PQLI) of 0.800 which is equal to the European average. As against this, Bihar and Uttar Pradesh without 30 per cent allocation in the same areas have managed a PQIL of just about 0.400.The most crucial parameter determining PQIL is matters associated with education. Countries such as Japan and South Korea have attained the status of miracle economies, as their governments have assigned the 'most faovourable status' to expenditure on education. Even within India, the high degree of social development in Kerala is largely due to a high proportion of budgetary allocation to education.

It is time for India, at national and State levels, to realize that accelerating the rate of development will depend more on human resources than on the financial resources. Education is a core sector for achieving the objective of employment, human resource development and bringing about much needed change in social environment leading to overall progress through efficient use of resources. An appropriate education system cultivates knowledge, skill, positive attitude, awareness and sense of responsibility towards rights and duties and imparts inner strength to face oppression, humiliation and inequality. (Ninth Five-year Plan, 1997-2002)

III

STRUCTURE OF HIGHER EDUCATION IN PUNJAB

The State of Punjab represents the typical case of higher levels of state income coexisting with lower levels of literacy. The State has been experiencing serious imbalance in terms of greater overall economic prosperity with lagged quality of human resources. The educational growth in the State is highly skewed. The level of education among the weaker sections, women, slum dwellers, rural folk, agricultural labourers, marginal and small farmers, and informal sector workers is very low. The crux of the problem is that the faster agricultural growth of the State has in fact camouflaged the limited progress of the State in the sphere of social sector. This situation necessitates making an in-depth analysis of public spending on education in the State keeping in view its own economic position and educational performance *vis-à-vis* that of other States.

The general socio-economic scenario in the State of Punjab exhibits complex relationship between economic growth and social sector development. Punjab State has been experiencing serious imbalance in terms of high income levels and laggard quality of human resources.

Reasonably high level State income co-exists with relatively moderate level of human resources when the latter have been measured in terms of educational and health standards. There is inadequate transfer of resources towards the improvement of the quality of human resources. The sustained high growth in the State over long period, much higher than the national average, has placed it with substantially higher level of per capita income not only from the national average but also from the good majority of the rest of the States in the country. The State has acquired the distinction of being the typical model of agrarian transformation not only within the country but also among the rest of the countries similarly placed. The State has an industrial sector built upon the small and tiny units, though concentrated in few urban pockets. The State has been the beneficiary of foreign remittances repatriated by the non-resident population of the State settled in advanced countries. The State attracts larger number of migratory labourers from the non-green revolution cum non-industrialized States of the country. Actually, the State has sustained noticeable economic prosperity and distanced itself from the number of States in the Country.

A person who is able to read and write with understanding in any language is recorded as literate. In Punjab during the last ten years literacy rate (Table 4.1) has been rising. As against 33.67 per cent in the year 1971, it has reached the level of 69.95 per cent. The decade of 1980s is characterized by a major jump in the literacy. It was 58.51 per cent in 1991 and it increased to 69.95 per cent in 2001, i.e., an increase of 11.44 per cent points during the last ten years. Gender-wise breakup of the literacy indicates that in the year 2001, female literacy stands at 63.55 per cent as against the same for male at 75.63 per cent. Relatively low female literacy in Punjab is really a matter of concern for the planners and academicians.

Table 4.1

Progress of Literacy in Punjab

Segment	Literacy in year			
	1971	1981	1991	2001
Person	33.67	40.86	58.51	69.95
Male	40.38	47.16	65.66	75.63
Female	25.90	33.69	50.41	63.55

Note: Excluding (0-6) years of age group.

Source: Statistical Abstract of Punjab, Chandigarh (Various Issues).

Over a period of time, the situation is improving. Punjab has fared well in reducing the gap between male and female literacy, which decreased from 15.25 per cent in 1991 to 12.08 per cent in 2001. There is also a noticeable change between urban and rural literacy (Table 4.2). The gap has significantly narrowed down in the last decade according to Census 2001. According to Census 2001, rural literacy is 65.16 per cent and urban literacy is 79.13 per cent. So the gap between urban and rural literacy has reduced from 19.31 per cent point in 1991 to 13.97 per cent points in 2001. But in spite of these positive trends, there are still 94.35 lakh illiterates in the State (Census of 2001).

Table 4.2

Area-wise Literacy Rate in Punjab (1991-2001)

Year	Literacy Rate		
	Rural	Urban	Total
1991	52.77	72.08	58.51
2001	65.16	79.13	69.95

Note: Excluding (0-6) years of age group.

Source: Census of India (Punjab), 1991-2001

It is a matter of great concern that in spite of having improved its literacy rate figure, the rank of Punjab has went down from the 12th position in 1971 to the 16th in 2001, when compared to other States and UTs in India. At present, Kerala has the highest literacy rate of 90.92 per cent while Bihar has the lowest of 47.53 per cent.

Table 4.3

States and Union Territories Ranked by Literacy Rate, 2001

State/URs	Literacy Rate	Rank by Literacy
1	2	3
Kerala	90.92	1
Mizoram	88.49	2
Lakshadweep	87.52	3
Goa	82.32	4
Delhi	81.82	5
Chandigarh	81.76	6
Pondicherry	81.49	7
Andaman & Nicobar Islands	81.18	8
Daman & Diu	81.09	9
Maharashtra	77.27	10
Himachal Pradesh	77.13	11
Tripura	73.66	12
Tamil Nadu	73.47	13
Uttranchal	72.28	14
Gujarat	69.97	15
Punjab	69.95	16
Sikkim	69.68	17
West Bengal	69.22	18
Manipur	68.87	19

(Contd...)

1	2	3
Haryana	68.59	20
Nagaland	67.11	21
Karnataka	67.04	22
Assam	64.28	24
Madhya Pradesh	64.11	25
Orissa	63.61	26
Meghalaya	63.31	27
Andhra Pradesh	61.11	28
Rajasthan	61.03	29
Dadra & Nagar Haveli	60.03	30
Uttar Pradesh	57.36	31
Arunachal Pradesh	54.74	32
Jammu & Kashmir	54.46	33
Jharkhand	54.13	34
Bihar	47.53	35

Source: Census of India, 2001.

Planned Outlay on Education in Punjab

The successive Five-year Plans have played a very significant role in shaping the educational policies and programmes of the government. The Ninth Five-year Plan treated education as the most crucial investment in human development. The thrust areas for educational development in the Ninth Plan included raising the quality of education at all levels, improving learner achievement, uplift of the educational status of disadvantaged groups including scheduled caste and scheduled tribe girls and disabled children, removing of regional disparities, vocationalization of education, updating/renewal of the curriculum to meet emerging challenges in information technology and support for the development of centers of excellence at the tertiary level.

Table 4.4

Outlay and Expenditure in different Five Year Plans on General Education

(Rs. In Lakh)

Plans	Approved outlay on education	Percentage of total outlay	Expenditure on education
Fourth Five-year Plan (1969-74)	2100.00	7.16	2307.69
Fifth Five-year Plan (1974-78)	4327.00	4.21	3056.43
Sixth Five-year Plan (1980-85)	5300.00	2.71	5470.58
Seventh Five-year Plan (1985-90)	7637.00	2.32	6371.27
Eighth Five-year Plan (1992-97)	21683.00	2.62	23714.82
Ninth Five-year Plan (1997-2002)	41310.49	2.89	60947.61
Tenth Five-year Plan (2002-2007)	141089.77	6.07	–

Source: Statistical Abstract of Punjab, (1970-2002).

The data reveal that the present outlay has come down to 2.89 per cent in the Ninth Plan from 7.16 per cent in the Fourth and 4.21 per cent in Fifth Plan. The percentage of the total outlay to the education sector had been consistently decreasing until the Seventh Plan. In the Eighth and the Ninth Five Year Plans, although there has been a marginal increase in the outlay, i.e., it increased to 2.62 per cent in the Eighth Plan and 2.89 per cent in the Ninth Plan, but the percentage is still very low as compared to the Fourth Plan and even the Fifth Plan. Hence, it is obvious that the education sector is not being given as much priority as it was given earlier. However, the expenditure during the Ninth Plan, i.e., from 1997 to 2000 has really exceeded the given outlay. Rs. 60,947.61 lakh has been spent on education in 1997-2001 as against the allotted amount of Rs. 41,310.49 lakh. The main reason was the implementation of the recommendations of the Fifth Pay Commission, wherein again the major amount was spent on salaries/State liabilities rather than educational development. In the Tenth Plan a major jump to Rs. 1,41,089.77 lakh is envisaged for the education sector and the State Government claims that besides meeting the State liabilities, during this Plan period, care is being taken to ensure that the money released is utilized to meet the objectives of development.

In spite of the fact that educational expenditure continues to be the highest item next only to defence, the resource gap for educational needs is still one of the major problems. Punjab is spending 2.88 per cent of the SGDP on education in comparison to 3.62 per cent at the national level. However, this percentage is really less, as there was a clear indication in the NPE 1986 that the investment on education should reach six per cent of the national income. Not only is the allocation for education very low, but according to present data, a large percentage is spent on salaries, leaving very little for development of education itself. Financing of secondary and higher education has however shown a declining trend from the Sixth Plan onwards; reflecting the priority to implement free and compulsory elementary education.

The major thrust area in the Tenth Five-year Plan is to meet the increased demand for secondary education. The main objective is to raise the enrolment of the population in the age group (18-23) in higher education from the present 6 per cent to 10 per cent by the end of the Tenth Plan period. The focus and strategies would be on increasing access; quality, adoption of State specific strategies, liberalization of higher education system; relevance including curriculum, vocationalisation, networking and information technology, distance education; convergence of formal, non-formal, distance and IT education institutions; increased private participation in establishing and running of colleges and deemed to be universities; research in frontier areas of knowledge and meeting challenges in the area of internationalization of Indian education.

Higher Education System in Punjab

In higher education, the State of Punjab has an elaborate higher education system that includes traditional humanities, science and arts colleges and the present day professional colleges. As per the *Statistical Abstract of Punjab, 2005*, presently there are five universities in the State; more than two hundred arts, science and commerce colleges; more than thirty colleges of engineering, technology and architecture; six medical colleges and a large number of teacher training education colleges. Since some new colleges have been opened in the recent past, hence figures of medical and teacher training colleges may be slightly higher than this reported figure.

The number of universities which (*Table 4.5*) was only three up to the decade of 1990's stands at five. Newly opened universities are a medical university, veterinary university, a law university and a technical university. Opening of some more specialized universities and some private universities is under consideration of the government. The multi-faculty colleges that were 122 in 1971, grew to 162 in 1980, to 171 in 1990 and finally to 212 in the year 2004. Number of girls' multi-faculty colleges has also significantly improved. As against a mere number of 37 in 1971, it has touched the mark of 79 in the year 2004. Number of engineering and technology colleges/ institutes was just three in the decades of 1970s, 80s and then 1990s. But the years 2000 onwards have witnessed a phenomenal growth and the number stands at more than thirty. New medical colleges have also opened up. Teacher training colleges, commonly called B.Ed. colleges, that were just less than twenty in the state are also likely to swell in a multiple number of existing one.

Thus the number of institutions has grown very fast in the state. A look on the number of teachers (*Table 4.6*) in institutions shows that in general the number of teachers

Table 4.5

Number of Recognized Institutions in Punjab

Year	Universities	Arts, Science Commerce and Home Science Colleges			Engineering Technology and Architecture Colleges	Medical Colleges	Teacher Training (B.Ed.) Colleges
	Total	Male	Female	Total	Total	Total	Total
1971	3	85	37	122	2	4	17
1980	3	110	52	162	3	5	18
1990	3	118	53	171	3	5	18
2000	5	131	73	204	16	6	22
2002	5	131	78	209	16	6	24
2003	5	131	78	209	16	6	23
2004	5	133	79	212	27	6	24

Source: *Statistical Abstract of Punjab*, 2005.

has not grown in synchronization with the number of institutions. When the number of universities in the State was three in 1990, the number of teachers was 507. Now when the universities are five in number, the teacher strength is 520 only. Partly, it is due to the fact that two of the newly opened universities are basically affiliating and examining bodies only and they do not give their own in-house courses. In the multi-faculty colleges the teacher strength has grown with the number of institutions. Same is the case with engineering and medical education. But in teacher training colleges, where teacher only is the basic input, the number of teachers has not grown in consonance with the number of institutions.

The higher education system of the State, initially a state planned and financed, has been thrown open to the private sector in the past decade. The government has started withdrawing from financing higher education and the higher education institutions are expected to be self-sustaining. As a result of this, there has been a drastic structural change in the higher education system of the state. Traditional multi-faculty arts, science, commerce and home science colleges have introduced many self financed job oriented courses.

Universities of the State, basically perceived to be the temples of higher learning and research, have also entered into the business of college education. Medical education and the teacher training education have also been thrown open to the private sector. Enhancing existing fee or charging exorbitant fees is a common phenomenon. In the name of paid/NRI/Management quota seats less qualified students replace the qualified intake of the institutions. The higher education in the state is characterized by the feature of exclusion of masses. The model of higher education has continuously excluded the rural and the poor. Rising salary component has pressurized the cut on library, equipment and other activities. Research and development is on no one's agenda. Resource mobilization, that too just a short

Table 4.6

Number of Teachers in Institutions of Punjab

Year	Universities	Arts, Science Commerce and Home Science Colleges			Engineering Technology and Architecture Colleges	Medical Colleges	Teacher Training (B.Ed.) Colleges
	Total	Male	Female	Total	Total	Total	Total
1971	155	2865	1066	3931	160	453	267
1980	398	3105	1604	4700	245	826	272
1990	507	3401	2653	6054	268	1106	255
2000	613	3421	3804	7225	1074	1364	394
2002	546	3382	4098	7480	1286	1141	379
2003	474	3270	4306	7576	1286	942	391
2004	520	3206	4453	7659	1330	1008	394

Source: *Statistical Abstract of Punjab*, 2005.

term, is the only objective. Long-term business of an institution is a function of its brand-image and a short-term business is to sell what has a market. Higher education system of the State has moved somewhat on the later option. All these problems have been further accentuated by the gradual state withdrawal from the State.

The State of Punjab, as such, has no strategic long-term plan for higher education. Every current wave of market demand is the only guide mark for investment. Millennium opening, characterized by information technology boom all around, led to mushrooming of information technology institutions. Many new institutions opened up and some of the existing one's replaced their traditional courses with new ones. Presently, the boom led education in teacher training is on the same lines. This impulsive response of the education system to short market demand surge leads to a massive mis-planned human resource orientation.

Research Related Education

In a growing and leading State such as Punjab, where thorough structural transformation of existing structure is need of the time; the research and development should have been the top most on the agenda. The numbers of students going in for research courses like M.Phil. and Ph.D. (Table 4.7) is negligible. It is less than even one per cent of the students who started their primary education years back. The drop-out rate is high. Instant market-driven courses are also one prime reason for the same. The number of students opting for M.Phil., has come drastically down because the course has been closed in many subjects due to less number of seekers for the programme. Otherwise also the course has not been linked to higher research degrees or job placement in the last few years. The number of female students is above the half mark. The larger number of female researchers is a function of their larger number in post graduate courses and their general objective of sticking to education.

Table 4.7

Number of Students in Research Courses in Punjab

Year	Ph.D.			M.Phil.		
	Male	Female	Total	Male	Female	Total
1971	12 (92.31)	1 (7.69)	13 (100.00)	–	–	–
1980	56 (54.90)	46 (45.10)	102 (100.00)	138 (49.64)	140 (50.36)	278 (100.00)
1990	74 (50.00)	74 (50.00)	148 (100.00)	263 (42.56)	355 (57.44)	618 (100.00)
2000	102 (37.50)	170 (62.50)	272 (100.00)	18 (26.09)	51 (73.91)	69 (100.00)
2002	80 (37.91)	131 (62.09)	211 (100.00)	40 (36.04)	71 (63.96)	111 (100.00)
2003	90 (46.39)	104 (53.61)	194 (100.00)	59 (40.97)	85 (59.03)	144 (100.00)
2004	140 (42.68)	188 (57.32)	328 (100.00)	38 (25.85)	109 (74.15)	147 (100.00)

Note: Figures in parentheses are percentages.

Source: Statistical Abstract of Punjab, 2005.

Caste-wise distribution research programmes is given in Table 4.8. Number of scheduled caste students in Ph.D. research that was 1.35 per cent in 1990 has touched the zero mark. In M.Phil. programme, historically the number of scheduled caste students has never crossed the mark of 7 per cent mark. This is primarily because of the higher cost of such education and the long duration of the programmes.

Post-Graduate Education

Major chunk of students in post graduate education in the state is in post graduate courses of arts, science and commerce. Number of students in post-graduation in engineering, medical and management education is very small.

As compared to Commerce, where the number of students is 1308, the number of students in science is almost double of it and number of students in arts is more than ten times of it (*Table 4.9*). In the temporal dimension, as compared to 4112 students in arts in 1971, the number has touched 5291 mark in 1990 and now it stands at 13,417 in the year 2004. As compared to the early seventies, there is a three-fold increase in it. Post graduation in science was negligible in 1970s. Only 359 students went for it at that time. The number of students in M.Sc. rose to 1136 in 1990 and touched 4234 in the year 2004. Thus in the last few decades there has been more than 10 times rise in M.Sc students' number. Number of students with commerce is also consistently improving. So in the past, as compared to arts courses, the student strength has significantly improved in the science and commerce courses, but still the number of students in post graduation in arts is quite high.

Table 4.8

Number of SC Students in Research Institutions of Punjab

Year	Ph.D.			M.Phil.		
	Male	Female	Total	Male	Female	Total
1971	0	0	0	0	0	0
1980	0	0	0	6 (4.35)	0	6 (2.16)
1990	1 (1.35)	1 (1.35)	2 (1.35)	10 (3.80)	7 (1.97)	17 (2.75)
2000	0	0	0	0	0	0
2002	0	0	0	0	0	0
2003	0	0	0	4 (6.78)	5 (5.88)	9 (6.25)
2004	0	0	0	0	0	0

Note: Figures in parentheses are percentages.

Source: *Statistical Abstract of Punjab*, 2005.

Table 4.9

Number of Students in Post-Graduate Courses in Institutions of Punjab

Year	M.A			M.Sc.			M.Com		
	Male	Female	Total	Male	Female	Total	Male	Female	Total
1971	2602 (63.28)	1510 (36.72)	4112 (100.00)	244 (67.97)	115 (32.03)	359 (100.00)	3 (100.00)	0 (0.00)	3 (100.00)
1980	2852 (48.86)	2985 (51.14)	5837 (100.00)	338 (51.45)	319 (48.55)	657 (100.00)	22 (81.48)	5 (18.52)	27 (100.00)
1990	2176 (41.13)	3115 (58.87)	5291 (100.00)	500 (44.01)	636 (55.99)	1136 (100.00)	61 (50.83)	59 (49.17)	120 (100.00)
2000	3421 (31.17)	7553 (68.83)	10974 (100.00)	580 (30.07)	1349 (69.93)	1929 (100.00)	153 (25.76)	441 (74.24)	594 (100.00)
2002	80 (37.91)	131 (62.09)	211 (100.00)	40 (36.04)	71 (63.96)	111 (100.00)			
2003	3242 (28.64)	8077 (71.36)	11319 (100.00)	865 (26.79)	2364 (73.21)	3229 (100.00)	237 (21.45)	868 (78.55)	1105 (100.00)
2004	3797 (28.30)	9620 (71.70)	13417 (100.00)	1187 (28.03)	3047 (71.97)	4234 (100.00)	240 (18.35)	1068 (81.65)	1308 (100.00)

Note: Figures in parentheses are percentages.

Source: Statistical Abstract of Punjab, 2005.

Percentage of female students going to arts post-graduate courses has drastically changed. Mere 36.72 per cent of the female students were in M.A. courses in 1971. It crossed half mark in early eighties and crossed 60 per cent mark in the decade of nineties. Now for the last few years the number of female students is more than seventy per cent of the total students. With minor variations, same is the behaviour pattern of M.Sc. students. Here also more than 70 per cent of the students are female students. Going to post graduate course in commerce, there used to be no female students in such courses in the 1970s. The female student strength in M.Com crossed fifty per cent mark in the early nineties decade and presently it is above the eighty per cent mark. Thus percentage of female students is showing the tendency to touch the three-fourth mark shortly.

Distribution of scheduled caste post-graduate students is given in Table 4.10. Number of scheduled caste students has been 8.89 per cent in arts courses; 5.72 per cent in science courses and 4.28 per cent in commerce course in the year 2004. Gender-wise break up of reserve category shows that number of students going to post-graduation in arts has been 11.80 per cent for males and 7.72 per cent in case of females. Similarly in science post-graduation courses, as against 9.01 per cent of male scheduled castes, only 4.43 per cent has been the females. But in case of commerce post graduation courses, percentage of the male students has been 3.75 per cent for males and 4.40 per cent for females. Thus against the scheduled caste reserved seats, in general, more of males are coming to post-graduate education than females in Punjab. Thus in post-graduate education in the state of Punjab number of females is consistently rising in arts, science and commerce and it is poised to touch the 75 per cent mark. But in case of scheduled caste category, the number of students availing reservation is still higher for males as compared to females. There needs to be done a lot for this deprived section of the society.

Table 4.10

Distribution of Scheduled Caste Students in Post-Graduate Courses in Institutions of Punjab

Year	M.A			M.Sc.			M.Com		
	Male	Female	Total	Male	Female	Total	Male	Female	Total
1971	171 (6.57)	20 (1.32)	191 (4.64)	0	0	0	0	0	0
1980	424 (14.87)	67 (2.24)	491 (8.41)	16 (4.73)	0	16 (2.44)	0	0	0
1990	446 (20.50)	233 (7.48)	679 (12.83)	27 (5.40)	11 (1.73)	38 (3.35)	11 (18.03)	0	11 (9.17)
2000	543 (15.83)	620 (8.21)	1163 (10.60)	48 (2.28)	52 (3.85)	100 (5.18)	28 (18.30)	22 (4.49)	50 (8.42)
2002	401 (13.55)	593 (8.04)	994 (9.62)	52 (8.09)	51 (2.86)	103 (4.25)	18 (8.37)	21 (2.36)	39 (3.53)
2003	415 (12.80)	598 (7.40)	1012 (8.94)	70 (8.09)	84 (3.55)	154 (4.77)	18 (7.59)	23 (2.65)	41 (3.71)
2004	448 (11.80)	743 (7.72)	1193 (8.89)	107 (9.01)	135 (4.43)	242 (5.72)	9 (3.75)	47 (4.40)	56 (4.28)

Note: Figures in parentheses are percentages.

Source: Statistical Abstract of Punjab, 2005.

Graduate Courses

Graduate courses are the feeding area for post-graduate courses. A look on absolute numbers shows that all the three streams are popular. Students are oddly distributed among the three streams, with a highest number of students in arts followed by science and commerce in order. As compared to 16,386 students in commerce in year 2004, the number of students in graduation in arts and science is 1,35,591 and 21,453 respectively (*Table 4.11*). In the past few years number of students going to science graduation has continuously improved but the number of students going for commerce has declined marginally. Number of students shows a mixed trend. Number of female students in B.A. courses is stable at 53 to 54 per cent mark but in case of B.Sc., the number of female students has touched the 62 per cent mark. On the other hand, in case of B. Com. the number of female students is stable around 44 to 46 per cent in the last one and a half decade.

The percentage of scheduled caste students in B.A., in 2004, is 11.76 per cent and there is a slight difference among male and female students (*Table 4.12*). It is 12.11 per cent for males as against 12.47 per cent for females. The percentage of scheduled caste students in 2004 in B.Sc. is 6.98 per cent; being 9.09 per cent for males and 5.67 per cent for females for the same year. In case of commerce, the number of scheduled caste students is 5.55 per cent of total while the males are 6.07 per cent and females are 4.93 per cent.

As compared to graduate stream, the post graduate system of the state shows that percentage of girl students in total students sharply increases in all streams of post graduation. In arts, it rises from 62 per cent to 71 per cent and in commerce it rises from 46 per cent to 82 per cent as soon as there is shift from graduation to post graduation. The reason behind this drastic change is that all the three traditional streams are not job-oriented. Male students in

Table 4.11

Number of Students in Graduate Courses in Institutions of Punjab

Year	B.A			B.Sc.			B.Com		
	Male	Female	Total	Male	Female	Total	Male	Female	Total
1971	34220 (67.50)	16480 (32.50)	50700 (100.00)	10467 (81.88)	2316 (18.12)	12783 (100.00)	1365 (99.85)	2 (0.15)	1367 (100.00)
1980	33436 (54.75)	27635 (45.25)	61071 (100.00)	7780 (69.62)	3395 (30.38)	11175 (100.00)	5162 (94.09)	324 (5.91)	5486 (100.00)
1990	26590 (43.98)	33867 (56.02)	60457 (100.00)	5175 (53.73)	4457 (46.27)	9632 (100.00)	5955 (68.69)	2714 (31.31)	8669 (100.00)
2000	56218 (45.61)	67037 (54.39)	123255 (100.00)	7207 (46.24)	8380 (53.76)	15587 (100.00)	11536 (53.50)	10027 (46.50)	21563 (100.00)
2002	62886 (46.42)	72596 (53.58)	135482 (100.00)	8322 (44.32)	10456 (55.68)	18778 (100.00)	10440 (55.60)	8336 (44.40)	18776 (100.00)
2003	60504 (45.74)	71767 (54.26)	132271 (100.00)	8861 (44.96)	10847 (55.04)	19708 (100.00)	9508 (54.36)	7982 (45.64)	17490 (100.00)
2004	61828 (45.60)	73763 (54.40)	135591 (100.00)	8219 (38.31)	13234 (61.69)	21453 (100.00)	8807 (53.75)	7579 (46.25)	16386 (100.00)

Note: Figures in parentheses are percentages.

Source: Statistical Abstract of Punjab, 2005.

Table 4.12

Number of SC Students in Graduate Courses in Institutions of Punjab

Year	B.A			B.Sc.			B.Com		
	Male	Female	Total	Male	Female	Total	Male	Female	Total
1971	2884 (8.43)	287 (1.74)	3171 (6.25)	339 (3.24)	11 (0.47)	350 (2.74)	21 (1.54)	0	21 (1.54)
1980	4631 (13.85)	1192 (4.31)	5823 (9.53)	358 (4.60)	86 (2.53)	444 (3.97)	148 (2.87)	3 (0.93)	151 (2.75)
1990	5013 (18.85)	2712 (8.01)	7725 (12.78)	419 (8.10)	156 (3.50)	575 (5.97)	256 (4.30)	53 (1.95)	309 (3.56)
2000	7245 (12.89)	6810 (10.16)	14055 (11.40)	497 (6.90)	387 (4.62)	884 (5.67)	749 (6.49)	418 (4.17)	1167 (5.41)
2002	7914 (12.58)	7308 (10.07)	15222 (11.24)	692 (8.32)	542 (5.18)	1234 (6.57)	624 (5.98)	428 (5.13)	1052 (5.60)
2003	7835 (12.95)	7783 (10.84)	15618 (11.81)	647 (7.30)	582 (5.37)	1265 (6.42)	662 (6.96)	373 (4.67)	1035 (5.92)
2004	7490 (12.11)	8459 (11.47)	15949 (11.76)	747 (9.09)	751 (5.67)	1498 (6.98)	535 (6.07)	374 (4.93)	909 (5.55)

Note: Figures in parentheses are percentages.

Source: Statistical Abstract of Punjab, 2005.

the State have a mindset of doing at least graduation and then shifting to newly started job-oriented courses in administration, management, computers and law and female stick to higher education to reach the research level.

Professional Courses

Professional courses related to engineering, technology, medical and education are relatively a new phenomena in the state. The number of engineering and technology students, which used to be less than 2000 till early nineties, has crossed the 17,000 mark. Right from the decade of 1970s till date the number of students in medical courses has grown to near 2760 in 2004 as against 2088 in 1970 (*Table 4.13*). The number of B.Ed. students (where still fresh data is awaited) has increased a lot. In engineering courses the number of female students that used to be just below eight per cent till early nineties has reached 21.24 per cent. The number of female students has become 52.68 per cent in 2004 as against 24.04 per cent in year 1970. In B.Ed. the number of female students has reached the mark of 73.84 per cent of total students. As such the professional courses are becoming equally popular among the female students.

Caste-wise analysis of the student data shows that much of the reservation facility has been availed by students in medical and teacher training. In medical courses more than 18 per cent of the students belong to scheduled caste category and in teacher training, this percentage stands at 16.37 per cent. Number of scheduled caste students going for engineering courses is only 7.03 per cent in 2004.In all the three cases, number of male students availing reservation is higher than that of females (*Table 4.14*).

Thus, this synoptic review indicates that the higher education is picking up in the State. The traditional graduation in arts, science or commerce is done by the students as a mandatory minimum qualification.

Table 4.13

Number of Students in Professional Courses in Institutions of Punjab

Year	B.E./B.Tech/B.Arch			M.B.B.S			B.Ed.		
	Male	Female	Total	Male	Female	Total	Male	Female	Total
1971	1378 (99.64)	5 (0.36)	1383 (100.00)	1586 (75.96)	502 (24.04)	2088 (100.00)	1243 (39.60)	1896 (60.40)	3139 (100.00)
1980	1676 (98.18)	31 (1.82)	1707 (100.00)	1629 (73.51)	587 (26.49)	2216 (100.00)	1009 (37.40)	1689 (62.60)	2698 (100.00)
1990	1943 (92.04)	168 (7.96)	2111 (100.00)	1312 (56.99)	990 (43.01)	2302 (100.00)	1007 (30.98)	2243 (69.02)	3250 (100.00)
2000	10787 (81.53)	2444 (18.47)	13231 (100.00)	1327 (52.81)	1186 (47.19)	2513 (100.00)	1079 (29.42)	2589 (70.58)	3668 (100.00)
2002	11348 (81.15)	2636 (18.85)	13984 (100.00)	1326 (50.21)	1315 (49.79)	2641 (100.00)	1154 (30.06)	2685 (69.94)	3839 (100.00)
2003	11348 (81.15)	2636 (18.85)	13984 (100.00)	1187 (47.52)	1311 (52.48)	2498 (100.00)	1018 (26.30)	2853 (73.70)	3871 (100.00)
2004	13439 (78.76)	3625 (21.24)	17064 (100.00)	1306 (47.32)	1454 (52.68)	2760 (100.00)	1095 (26.16)	3090 (73.84)	4185 (100.00)

Note: Figures in parentheses are percentages.

Source: *Statistical Abstract of Punjab*, 2005.

Table 4.14

Number of SC Students in Professional Courses in Institutions of Punjab

Year	B.E./B.Tech/B.Arch			M.B.B.S			B.Ed.		
	Male	Female	Total	Male	Female	Total	Male	Female	Total
1971	25 (1.81)	0	25 (1.81)	81 (5.11)	20 (3.98)	101 (4.84)	96 (7.72)	25 (1.32)	121 (3.85)
1980	109 (6.50)	0	109 (6.39)	333 (20.44)	47 (8.01)	380 (17.15)	274 (27.16)	121 (7.16)	395 (14.64)
1990	308 (15.85)	6 (3.57)	314 (14.87)	352 (26.83)	138 (13.94)	490 (21.29)	201 (19.96)	187 (8.34)	388 (11.94)
2000	1110 (10.29)	153 (6.26)	1263 (9.55)	258 (19.44)	207 (17.45)	465 (18.50)	272 (25.21)	449 (17.34)	721 (19.66)
2002	1191 (10.50)	196 (7.44)	1387 (9.92)	261 (19.68)	232 (17.64)	493 (18.67)	279 (24.18)	464 (17.28)	743 (19.35)
2003	1191 (10.50)	196 (7.44)	1387 (9.92)	153 (12.89)	180 (13.73)	333 (13.33)	215 (21.12)	434 (15.21)	469 (16.77)
2004	1006 (7.49)	193 (5.32)	1199 (7.03)	244 (18.68)	261 (17.95)	505 (18.30)	251 (22.92)	434 (14.05)	685 (16.37)

Note: Figures in parentheses are percentages.

Source: Statistical Abstract of Punjab, 2005.

After graduation male students go in for job-oriented courses and females stick to post graduation of some stream. If graduation system of the state is synchronized in tune with the pre-requisites of job-oriented post-graduate courses, the system can generate more competencies and become relevant. There is an urgent need of the time to make the current higher education system to be more inclusive in terms of price and space.

Cost of College Education

As already said that there is an urgent need to maximize the efficiency of inputs in the education sector and thereby eliminate the wastage of precious resources. Education sector is faced with the challenge of raising the effectiveness of utilization of available resources. In the regime of privatization, a system requires a maximization of revenue and minimization of the cost. Thus the economic analysis of cost and the cost recovery in college education is the need of the hour. In this context, the following chapter analyses the various aspects of cost and cost recovery in college education of Punjab. The chapter is divided into four sections. Accordingly, section first deals with broad analysis of the sample; section two analyses the recurring cost; section three elaborates the recurring cost recovery pattern; and the last section explores the behaviour of non-recurring expenditure.

I

BROAD ANALYSIS OF THE SAMPLE

The study covers 90 colleges of the state of Punjab in all. It is more than forty per cent of the population of such colleges of the state. The sample is composed of 26 government colleges; 42 private aided colleges and 22 unaided colleges (*Table 5.1*). Area-wise distribution of the sample is indicative of the fact that there are 43 colleges in the urban area, 17 in semi-urban area and 30 in the rural area. The average student-strength of government colleges, being 1354, is highest as compared to 1313 in case of private aided colleges and the same being 511 in case of private unaided colleges. Within the three ownership categories, the range of variation is very vast. The average strength varies from 240 to 5010 in case of government colleges; from 355 to 5090 in case of private aided colleges and from mere 89 to 1416 in case of private unaided colleges in the state. Thus most of the unaided colleges of the state are relatively small colleges. Further, the strength-wise big colleges are in the urban area; medium colleges are in the semi-urban area and the small colleges are in the rural area. The sample clearly indicates that the aided college education, both government and privately owned in the state is heavily biased in the favour of urban area and the rich. Such a model of higher education has continuously excluded the rural and the poor.

Composition of Output

Composition of output, i.e., the student strength, has also a strong bearing on the cost structure of college education. Multi-faculty colleges are still operating in a traditional set up of humanities followed by science, commerce and other professional courses in order of strength. Still 67.93 per cent of the total student strength belongs to arts courses (*Table 5.2*). Share of science students' strength is 15.74 and that of commerce is 10.66 per cent. The much talked about computer and management courses are just six per cent. In the wake of cut in aids, college education diversified into lucrative business options such as management and computer courses. Much of this effort has been done by private aided followed by unaided colleges.

Table 5.1

Distribution of Number of Colleges and Student Strength in Punjab

College Category	No. of Colleges	Average Strength	Range	
			Minimum	Maximum
Ownership-wise				
Government	26	1354	240	5010
Private Aided	42	1313	355	5090
Private Unaided	22	511	89	1416
Location-wise				
Urban	43	1620	240	5090
Semi-Urban	17	816	234	1999
Rural	30	602	89	1697
Size-wise				
Small	22	323	89	411
Medium	46	771	414	1537
Big	22	2599	1566	5090
Total	**90**	**1129**	**89**	**5090**

Source: Primary data.

Both government and aided colleges have experimented new courses for cost recovery within traditional framework of retaining arts, science and commerce courses. But the unaided colleges have skipped science and commerce courses and have directly jumped from arts and humanities to the professional courses. Most of the professional courses have been set up in the urban area colleges and that too by the big sized colleges. Thus, the professional courses have favoured large size, urban area and aided category institutions. This transition has again skipped the rural small-sized and unaided section of the college education.

Table 5.2

Course-wise Distribution of Students' Strength in College Education in Punjab

Type of College	Arts	Science	Com-merce	Comp-uter	Manage-ment	Total
Ownership-wise						
Government	68.99	18.02	9.77	3.12	0.10	100.00
Pvt. Aided	64.43	16.42	12.02	5.51	1.63	100.00
Pvt. Unaided	81.67	5.33	6.85	5.85	0.30	100.00
Location-wise						
Urban	63.60	17.65	12.17	5.62	0.95	100.00
Semi-Urban	71.55	17.26	9.57	0.78	0.84	100.00
Rural	81.60	7.31	5.76	4.30	1.03	100.00
Size-wise						
Small	92.19	2.41	1.94	3.47	0.00	100.00
Medium	78.71	7.98	9.42	2.90	0.99	100.00
Big	60.65	20.34	12.41	5.51	1.08	100.00
Total	**67.93**	**15.74**	**10.66**	**4.72**	**0.95**	**100.00**

Source: Primary data

Nature of Teaching Staff

Table 5.3 gives the average number of teachers per college in the State of Punjab. Ownership-wise analysis is indicative of the fact that private unaided colleges have on an average 20 teachers per college and government colleges and private aided colleges have almost more than double of this strength. There is a slight difference between government colleges and aided colleges as far as the teaching staff per college is concerned. In the private unaided colleges category relatively low co-efficient of variation (45.72%) shows that colleges in this category behave almost in the same manner. But the high value of the coefficient of variation of the range of 84.69 per cent and 89.36 per cent underscores the fact that there is a wide variation among the government college category and among the private aided colleges category. Same behaviour pattern is displayed by significant value of F given by analysis of variance (F=4.048)

Table 5.3

Distribution of Average Number of Teachers in Colleges of Punjab

Type of College	Average No. of Teachers	Coefficient of Variation (%)	F-Statistics
Ownership-wise			
Government	45	84.69	
Private Aided	44	89.36	
Private Unaided	20	45.72	4.048*
Location-wise			
Urban	54	81.15	
Semi-urban	30	48.94	
Rural	21	69.53	9.917*
Size-wise			
Small	15	36.21	
Medium	26	43.49	
Big	74	54.94	47.330*
Total	**39**	**92.63**	–

* Significant at 5%; ** Significant at 1%.

Source: Calculated

Location-wise analysis of colleges in Punjab highlights that from the teaching staff strength point of view urban colleges are the biggest ones and rural colleges are the smallest. Average teaching staff strength in urban colleges is 54; in semi-urban colleges it is 30; and in rural areas it is just 21. There is a wide variation in staff strength as far as individual type of location categories is concerned. The high value of coefficient of variation points to this fact. So the rural area colleges are in a disadvantaged situation as far as number of teachers per institution is concerned. Size wise analysis of average teaching staff strength gives the expected behaviour. Size wise big colleges have large number of teachers and smaller sized colleges have lesser number of teachers. The teaching staff strength in small colleges of Punjab is 15; medium sized colleges have 26 and in big colleges have 74.

Further analysis of Table 5.4 shows that in terms of nature of employment most of the teachers working on permanent basis are located in government colleges. However, the following table shows that the private aided and private unaided colleges are depending upon teaching staff on temporary or ad hoc basis. Most of this temporary and ad hoc staff is associated with colleges of semi-urban or rural area colleges. Size of the colleges does not affect this distribution. The above analysis shows that private unaided, rural and small sized colleges are characterized by poor teaching staff strength. But on the other hand government colleges, urban area colleges and the large sized colleges are in an advantaged position as far as teaching staff strength is concerned. Further the faculty on permanent basis is available in government colleges and colleges situated in the urban areas. Private colleges and the colleges situated in semi-urban or rural areas are running the system on the basis of temporary and ad hoc basis appointed staff.

Table 5.5 shows that private aided colleges depend more on temporary staff as compared to government and private unaided colleges. But there is not a significant variation among government, private unaided and private aided colleges. Similarly, location-wise also there is not much variation among urban, semi-urban and rural colleges. As far as size-wise classification is concerned, big colleges employ larger number of temporary staff and this significant variation is very much obvious from the values of coefficient of variation and analysis of variance (F= 14.415). This variation is merely because of the fact that big sized colleges have more enrolment and to cater to the needs of their strength, these colleges are required to employ more teachers.

Table 5.4

Distribution of Average Number of Permanent Teachers in Colleges of Punjab

Type of College	Average No. of Permanent Teachers	Coefficient of Variation (%)	F-Statistics
Ownership-wise			
Government	32	95.56	
Private Aided	30	93.54	
Private Unaided	12	53.76	4.3*
Location-wise			
Urban	37	88.55	
Semi-urban	20	58.58	
Rural	13	76.52	9.07*
Size-wise			
Small	10	42.39	
Medium	18	54.51	
Big	50	65.42	33.21**
Total	**26**	**56.63**	–

* Significant at 5%; ** Significant at 1%.

Source: Primary Data.

Thus the college education in Punjab is operating on temporary gap filling arrangement as far as teaching staff is concerned. In the present phase of competition such an approach needs to be thoroughly debated upon.

Table 5.5

Distribution of Average Number of Temporary Teachers in Colleges of Punjab

Type of College	Average No. of Temporary Teachers	Coefficient of Variation (%)	F-Statistics
Ownership-wise			
Government	13	102.27	
Private Aided	14	125.64	
Private Unaided	08	63.89	1.704
Location-wise			
Urban	17	121.76	
Semi-urban	10	73.34	
Rural	08	87.81	2.701
Size-wise			
Small	05	59.00	
Medium	08	10.00	
Big	24	91.00	14.415**
Total	**13**	**88.91**	–

** Significant at 1%.

Source: Primary Data.

Student-Teacher Ratio

Student teacher ratio has also a very strong bearing on cost and recovery system of an institution. Student-teacher ratio in government colleges is 33.96, in private aided colleges it is 32.21 and in private unaided colleges it is 25.95 in Punjab (*Table 5.6*). In case of location-wise distribution of data urban colleges have the highest teacher-student ratio, followed by rural and semi-urban in order. Size-wise the big colleges have student-teacher ratio as 35.80, medium sized colleges have 32.36 and small colleges have 21.40. Thus in terms of student-teacher ratio the government colleges, the urban colleges and the big sized colleges are characterized by a relatively higher ratio. Private unaided colleges, rural colleges and small sized colleges are characterized by relatively lower ratio. As per the well expected norm of 40 students per teacher, student teacher ratio in colleges of Punjab on an average is on the lower side, thereby highlighting the unutilized capacity of existing teaching staff strength.

Table 5.6

Student-Teacher Ratio in Colleges of Punjab

Type of College	Average Ratio (%)	Coefficient of Variation (%)	F-Statistics
Ownership-wise			
Government	33.96	54.85	
Private Aided	32.21	41.67	
Private Unaided	25.95	37.69	1.970
Location-wise			
Urban	32.93	54.49	
Semi-urban	27.76	28.21	
Rural	30.63	39.21	0.768
Size-wise			
Small	21.40	37.74	
Medium	32.36	32.38	
Big	35.80	56.40	4.104*
Total	**29.85**	**44.51**	–

* Significant at 5%

Source: Primary Data.

The student-teacher ratio at a disaggregated level highlights more interesting facts (Table 5.7). In total there are 49 colleges, which have student-teacher ratio ranging from 10 to 30 and 37 colleges, have the student-teacher ratio ranging from 30 to 60. Only 3 colleges have student-teacher ranging from 60 to 90. There are 18 colleges in all which are exceeding the well accepted norm of 40 students per teacher.

Table 5.7

Distribution of Student-Teacher Ratio (Per cent) in Colleges of Punjab

Number of Students per Teacher	Frequency
10-30	49
30-60	37
60-90	3
90-120	1

Source: Primary data.

Thus, the general description of the sample highlights that average college education of the state lacks any vision or planning. The system, by virtue of unplanned evolution, is pro-urban area and has pro-private tendencies. To be more inclusive and evenly spread, the system of college education needs to be planned in strategic terms with a long-term vision.

II

RECURRING COST ANALYSIS

Percentage distribution of recurring cost (*Table 5.8*) is indicative of the fact that salaries component forms a major chunk of recurring cost in the state of Punjab. On the whole 92.97 per cent of the total recurring cost goes to the salaries alone. In the present phase of competition, library, equipment, free-ships and other consumables also do matter a lot. All these components are just seven per cent of the total recurring expenditure. Just 0.15 per cent of total recurring expenditure is spent on library. Almost the same magnitude goes for maintenance of furniture. In the list of items other than salaries, electricity consumption is the major head of expenditure. In percentage terms, it comes out to be 1.85 per cent. Building maintenance share in the

Table 5.8

Composition of Recurring Cost in Colleges of Punjab

Type of College	Total Salary	Library	Furniture	Building	Electricity	Lab Equip.	Vehicles	Sports	Scholarships	Others	Total Recurr. Cost
Ownership-wise											
Government	96.90	0.05	0.07	0.40	0.70	0.32	0.05	0.59	0.77	0.15	100.00
Pvt. Aided	91.02	0.21	0.22	1.55	2.49	0.74	0.53	0.84	1.17	1.23	100.00
Pvt. Unaided	86.03	0.23	0.19	1.65	3.38	0.99	4.56	0.56	1.66	0.75	100.00
Location-wise											
Urban	93.83	0.11	0.16	1.07	1.54	0.54	0.24	0.85	1.00	0.66	100.00
Semi-urban	92.43	0.29	0.16	1.38	1.60	0.76	0.30	0.48	1.07	1.53	100.00
Rural	89.33	0.24	0.14	1.09	3.55	0.69	2.68	0.31	1.26	0.72	100.00
Size-wise											
Small	92.98	0.16	0.18	1.09	2.33	0.46	0.56	0.48	1.04	0.73	100.00
Medium	90.36	0.31	0.17	1.34	2.92	0.70	1.82	0.51	1.32	0.56	100.00
Big	93.69	0.10	0.16	1.05	1.49	0.59	0.29	0.82	0.97	0.85	100.00
All	92.97	0.15	0.16	1.11	1.85	0.59	0.61	0.73	1.05	0.78	100.00

Source: Calculated.

total recurring cost stands at 1.11 per cent for the overall sample under consideration. Scholarships and other free-ships cost 1.05 per cent of the recurring outlay. Thus tight budget position of colleges in the State of Punjab leaves no space for expenditure on some of the important heads of inputs like library, furniture and building maintenance, equipment maintenance, consumables, extra-curricular activities and financial support to the needy and deserving ones.

Going to disaggregate level, analysis highlights some interesting facts. Ownership-wise analysis of percentage distribution of recurring cost shows that salary component share is highest in case of government colleges (96.90%). It is followed by private aided (91.02%) and private unaided (86.03 per cent) respectively. Thus, the first victim of government withdrawal from education is the salary structure of both teaching and non-teaching community. Thus movement from government to aided private and then to private unaided leads to a continuous slide down in the salary share. Private unaided staff, both teaching and non-teaching is ill-paid in comparison to the other two. Higher salary component in government colleges has left just negligible money of 3.10 per cent for all other recurring components. It has left just 0.05 per cent of the total recurring expenditure for library. Furniture, building maintenance and the vehicles share is also relatively low. With decrease of salary share component in government aided colleges as compared to government colleges, almost all the components have relatively improved. Same is the case of government unaided colleges. Private unaided colleges spend relatively bigger share on building maintenance, library upkeep, vehicle operations, consumables and free-ships, etc.

Location-wise analysis of the per cent distribution of recurring cost highlights the finer insights into the process. Higher salary share colleges are mostly in the urban area colleges. A movement away from urban to semi-urban and then to rural area leads to reduction in the salary share. As compared to urban area colleges' salary share of 93.83 per cent, the salary share in rural area colleges is 89.33 per cent. Due to this decrease in share, the released space has generally been shared by vehicles and electricity consumption in case of rural colleges and by building maintenance in case of semi-urban area colleges.

Size-wise analysis of composition of recurring cost underscores the fact that higher salary share is displayed by big sized colleges, it is 93.69 per cent as compared to 90.36 per cent in case of medium sized colleges and 92.98 per cent in case of small sized colleges. The pressure on non-salary components is evenly distributed among the other heads of expenditure with minor exceptions.

So, the salary component share in recurring expenditure is the highest in case of big sized government colleges located in urban areas. As the size has increased and as the movement has been from the country to the city side, there should have been enhanced share of library, building maintenance, vehicle operations, consumables, equipment maintenance, sports and free-ships. But all these items have been the first victim of state support withdrawal or support constraint. The big infrastructure created in the past are getting deteriorated or becoming unserviceable only because of lack of availability of funds for repair and maintenance. Some of the renowned institutions in sports, free-ships and extra-curricular activities have gone into total fade-out in this area due to lack of funds. The pressure on the funds has left the college education system to mean only the lecture delivery system and nothing more than this. The beneficiaries of current transformation are urban and the big sized colleges.

Total salary bill and its distribution among teaching and non-teaching staff (*Table 5.9*) shows that for the entire sample 71.90 per cent of salary bill goes to teaching and

Table 5.9

Composition of Salary Cost in Colleges of Punjab (Per cent)

Type of College	Teaching			Non-Teaching			Total Salary
	Basic Salary	Allowances	Total Salary	Basic Salary	Allowances	Total Salary	
Ownership-wise							
Government	53.79	10.83	64.62	29.67	5.71	35.38	100.00
Pvt. Aided	67.34	8.98	76.32	20.71	2.97	23.68	100.00
Pvt. Unaided	69.14	12.23	81.37	15.04	3.59	18.63	100.00
Location-wise							
Urban	62.02	9.49	71.52	24.36	4.12	28.48	100.00
Semi-Urban	65.06	10.17	75.23	20.64	4.12	24.77	100.00
Rural	59.06	11.87	70.93	27.98	4.09	29.07	100.00
Size-wise							
Small	62.68	11.04	73.72	20.99	5.29	26.28	100.00
Medium	61.53	11.42	72.95	22.62	4.43	27.05	100.00
Big	61.99	9.36	71.35	24.79	3.86	28.65	100.00
All	61.97	9.92	71.90	23.99	4.12	28.10	100.00

Source: Calculated.

the rest of 28.10 per cent goes to non-teaching component. Teaching salary component is highest (81.37%) in case of private unaided colleges. It is followed by private aided (76.32%) and government colleges (64.62%). This implies that private institutions of the state manage their salary budget by keeping a check on number of non-teaching employees and paying less to them as compared to government colleges. This cut in salary bill of non-teaching staff is both in terms of salary and number of employees. The private colleges operate the system with relatively lesser staff strength. The urban, Semi-urban and rural area colleges depict almost a similar behaviour with minor exceptions. Similarly the size of the institution also does not alter much to the composition of salary budget.

Salary Cost

As already said salary component, especially salary of the teaching staff is the major component of the recurring expenditure. Salary per teacher (*Table 5.10*) is highest in government colleges, followed by salary of teachers in private aided and private unaided colleges in order. The average annual salary per teacher is to the tune of Rs. 2.30 lakhs per year in government colleges; Rs. 1.91 lakhs in private aided colleges and just Rs. 1.03 lakhs in private unaided colleges. So a teacher in a government college gets more than the double of what a teacher gets in a private unaided college and a teacher in private unaided colleges is getting slightly less than the double of it. Relatively lower values of coefficient of variation prove that the variations in the individual type of colleges on the basis of ownership are not much. Analysis of variance shows that there is a significant difference in the average total salary per teacher in the three types of institutions.

Area-wise analysis shows that there is not much difference between semi-urban and the rural area colleges as far as the salary per teacher is concerned, but the salary in urban areas is slightly higher than the other two categories. Statistically speaking the difference between the three types of colleges as far as salary per teacher is concerned is not significant (F=1.754).

Size-wise the big colleges pay a higher salary, i.e., Rs. 2.08 lakhs, but the small and medium colleges pay Rs. 1.66 and 1.69 lakhs respectively. These salary differentials on the basis of the size of the college are not statistically significant (F=2.293). In the colleges of Punjab the salary differentials are the function of ownership type only and location or size of the institution has an insignificant affect.

Table 5.10

Distribution of Total Salary (Teaching Staff) in Colleges of Punjab

Type of College	Average Salary (Rs.)	Coefficient of Variation (%)	F-Statistics
Ownership-wise			
Government	229928	36.38	
Private Aided	190690	38.75	
Private Unaided	102858	45.58	18.975**
Location-wise			
Urban	198161	43.99	
Semi-urban	162811	40.06	
Rural	165376	53.58	1.754
Size-wise			
Small	165505	53.10	
Medium	168561	43.24	
Big	207600	42.73	2.293
Total	**193283**	**44.65**	–

** Significant at 1%.

Source: Primary Data.

Almost the same trend is observed in case of distribution of salary (*Table 5.11*) non-teaching staff. Salary per non-teaching staff member is highest in the government colleges followed by salary of the same in private aided and private unaided colleges respectively.

Table 5.11

Distribution Salary (Non-Teaching Staff) in Colleges of Punjab

Type of College	Average Salary (Rs.)	Coefficient of Variation (%)	F-Statistics
Ownership-wise			
Government	106752	44.80	
Private Aided	52944	82.05	
Private Unaided	26184	72.65	24.837**
Location-wise			
Urban	68640	80.08	
Semi-Urban	45624	82.67	
Rural	61584	78.34	1.255
Size-wise			
Small	61152	73.33	
Medium	52848	84.44	
Big	71808	82.34	1.048
Total	**66131**	**80.65**	–

** Significant at 1%.

Source: Primary Data.

Analysis of variance proves that there is a significant difference in the total salary per non-teaching staff members in the three types of institutions. Area-wise and size-wise variation between the three types of colleges is not statistically significant. Salary in urban colleges is more as compared to the other two categories. It could be because of the reason that generally large number of big sized colleges is located in urban areas and moreover urban colleges have more strength also. If we look at the number of teaching and non-teaching staff, comparatively large number of teaching and non-teaching staff is employed in big colleges than in medium and small colleges. So size-wise, big colleges pay a higher salary than medium and small sized colleges.

Basic salary per teaching and non-teaching staff person as given in (*Table 5.12*) and (*Table 5.13*) displays almost the same behaviour pattern as shown by total salary per teacher analyzed above. This implies variations in total salary, which is function of basic salary, are perfectly inconsonance with each other.

Table 5.12

Distribution of Basic Salary (Teaching Staff) in Colleges of Punjab

Type of College	Average Basic Salary (Rs.)	Coefficient of Variation (%)	F-Statistics
Ownership-wise			
Government	189716	39.59	
Private Aided	166511	41.33	
Private Unaided	87616	50.33	15.298**
Location-wise			
Urban	171393	48.11	
Semi-urban	138950	40.62	
Rural	137385	52.10	2.186
Size-wise			
Small	140411	54.06	
Medium	141801	42.92	
Big	179575	46.79	2.600
Total	**56659**	**85.62**	–

Source: Primary Data.

** Significant at 1%.

Allowances

Next component of salary is the allowances, dearness allowance being the major allowance. Average amount of allowances per teacher in government colleges is Rs. 40,212; in private aided colleges Rs. 24,179 and in private unaided colleges it is Rs. 15,242 per teacher. There is no significant difference in the allowances as far as the location is concerned or the size of the college is concerned.

Table 5.13

Distribution of Basic Salary (Non-Teaching Staff) in Colleges of Punjab

Type of College	Average Basic Salary (Rs.)	Coefficient of Variation (%)	F-Statistics
Ownership-wise			
Government	88248	48.31	
Private Aided	45456	87.16	
Private Unaided	21072	76.00	20.859**
Location-wise			
Urban	57360	86.20	
Semi-urban	37896	81.09	
Rural	51864	78.69	1.175
Size-wise			
Small	48696	70.70	
Medium	44232	85.50	
Big	62640	88.32	1.411
Total	**56659**	**85.62**	–

** Significant at 1%.

Source: Primary Data.

Hence the teaching staff in government colleges gets higher allowances and the teachers in private unaided colleges get relatively lower amount of allowances. The amount of allowances given to the teachers of private unaided colleges is negligible. Private unaided college teacher are paid just one third of the allowances that are being paid in government colleges. This cut definitely affects the living conditions and efficiency of the concerned staff. Privatization of higher education in Punjab has lead to a sharp cut in the allowances being paid to the teaching staff. Location-wise and size-wise differentials in allowances are because of theskewed strength of employees in the institutions.

Table 5.14

Distribution of Allowances (Teaching Staff) in Colleges of Punjab

Type of College	Average Allowances (Rs.)	Coefficient of Variation (%)	F-Statistics
Ownership-wise			
Government	40212	66.65	
Private Aided	24179	55.97	
Private Unaided	15242	37.49	12.691**
Location-wise			
Urban	26768	47.78	
Semi-urban	23860	62.26	
Rural	27991	101.08	0.233
Size-wise			
Small	25094	79.06	
Medium	26760	89.84	
Big	28025	49.24	0.162
Total	**27357**	**76.24**	–

** Significant at 1%.

Source: Primary Data.

A look on the allowances being paid to the non-teaching staff in Punjab underscores the fact that on an average the non-teaching employee gets Rs. 18,504 as allowances in addition to the basic salary. But for the private aided and private unaided category colleges it is Rs. 7,488 and Rs. 5,112 respectively (*Table 5.15*). Location-wise as compared to the other two categories, the employees working in urban area colleges are paid relatively higher allowances. Allowances per employee are relatively higher in small colleges because of bare minimum non-teaching employees.

Table 5.15

Distribution of Allowances (Non-Teaching Staff) in Colleges of Punjab

Type of College	Average Allowances (Rs.)	Coefficient of Variation (%)	F-Statistics
Ownership-wise			
Government	18504	58.85	
Private Aided	7488	136.85	
Private Unaided	5112	74.28	14.930**
Location-wise			
Urban	11280	112.23	
Semi-urban	7728	97.16	
Rural	9720	93.42	0.669
Size-wise			
Small	12456	116.11	
Medium	8616	100.91	
Big	9168	81.29	1.098
Total	**9472**	**105.69**	–

Source: Primary Data.

** Significant at 1%.

Recurring Cost per Unit

Total recurring cost per student is a best measure of average cost. Total recurring cost per student in government colleges is Rs. 12,413. It is Rs. 10,000 in case of aided and Rs. 6453 in unaided colleges. So the government colleges are spending almost double and private aided are spending almost one and a half times as compared to the unaided colleges in the state. The variations in the cost are relatively low in case of government colleges. This wide difference in total recurring cost per student in three types of colleges is displayed by analysis of variance also. (F= 7.333) (*Table 5.16*).

Table 5.16

Distribution of Recurring Cost per Unit in Colleges of Punjab

Type of College	Average Recurring Cost (Rs.)	Coefficient of Variation	F-Statistics
Ownership-wise			
Government	12413	38.12	
Private Aided	10000	63.13	
Private Unaided	6453	54.15	7.333**
Location-wise			
Urban	10714	62.60	
Semi-urban	8767	49.76	
Rural	9163	49.84	0.998
Size-wise			
Small	10112	46.70	
Medium	8752	53.75	
Big	10624	67.90	0.844
Total	**10134**	**55.62**	–

** Significant at 1%.

Source: Primary Data.

Location wise analysis of total recurring cost of students shows that higher cost is associated with urban areas, followed by rural area and semi-urban area colleges. This difference in recurring cost per student is not statistically significant as far as the location is concerned (F= 0.998). Same is the case of recurring cost when viewed according to the size of the colleges (F=0.844). Size-wise, the medium sized colleges are operating at a lower recurring cost per unit as compared to the big and the small sized colleges. Hence in the state the private, medium sized and semi-urban category colleges are operating at a relative lower recurring cost per unit. But, this cost efficiency, should not be mistaken to mean the operational or technical efficiency of the system.

Selected Correlates of Unit Cost

As per economic logic total output is a prime determinant of the cost and revenue of a unit. All cost components should be positively or negatively related to it depending on the scale and size of operations. Total salary, the major component of cost, depicts this relationship as expected (*Table 5.17*).

Table 5.17

Correlation of Total Student Strength with Selected Variables

Type of College	Total Salary (Teaching)	Total Salary (Non-teaching)	Total Cost	Unit Cost
Ownership-wise				
Government	0.862**	0.693**	0.850**	-0.324
Private Aided	0.784**	0.726**	0.796**	0.031
Private Unaided	0.441**	0.322	0.490*	-0.278
Area-wise				
Urban	0.777**	0.653**	0.792**	-0.003
Semi-Urban	0.770**	0.671**	0.797**	0.134
Rural	0.695**	0.411**	0.698**	-0.227
All	0.808**	0.707**	0.824**	0.041

* Significant at 1 per cent level.

** Significant at 5 per cent level.

Source: Calculated.

For the entire sample under consideration the correlation between total student strength and the total salary cost is 0.808 and is significant at one per cent level of significance. The results at disaggregated level are indicative of the fact that high and statistically significant correlation holds for both government and private aided colleges' categories. In case of private unaided colleges' category, no doubt, the correlation is positive and is statistically significant at one per cent level of significance but the correlation is relatively poor as compared to the other two categories. Hence, the salary bill is a positive and significant function of student strength in Punjab. Relatively weaker relation of students' strength with salary bill underscores the fact that private unaided colleges are operating the system either at lower teaching staff strength or by paying lesser salaries.

A look on the relation of total student strength with the non-teaching salary component shows that the relation is positive and statistically significant at one per cent level of significance for the total sample, in the government colleges and in the private aided colleges' categories. In case of private unaided colleges, although, the relation is positive but it is statistically insignificant. This implies that the private unaided colleges in the state operate the larger systems with relatively poorer strength of non-teaching or relatively ill-paid staff. The same holds true in case of relation of total output and the total cost. The relation is positive and statistically significant at a very low level of significance. In Punjab the total cost of college education is a positive function of output.

Logically the relation of unit cost or the average cost with total output can be negative, zero or positive depending on the position on average cost curve at which a particular institution is operating. Decreasing average cost in relation to output indicates the fact that the organization is approaching the minimum cost level, and vice-versa implies that the organization has crossed the minimum cost level. The relation of total student strength with unit cost is positive but statistically insignificant for the total sample and the private unaided category. On the other hand, the relation is negative but statistically insignificant in case of government and unaided colleges. Hence, the average cost for Punjab in general and for private unaided colleges in particular has just crossed the minimum cost level but the government colleges and private unaided colleges are approaching this level.

Area-wise correlation of total student strength with the salary (both teaching and non-teaching), total cost and the unit cost displays almost similar behaviour pattern as above except that now the relatively weaker but significant correlations are associated with rural area. This implies that increasing student strength has led to increase in salary in both urban and semi-urban area colleges but not to the same extent in rural areas. Thus in the present phase of privatization the victims of this onslaught are unaided private institutions and institutions located in the rural areas.

The correlation between total recurring cost and the total student enrollment has come up to be as expected (0.824**; n=90). It is positive and statistically significant at 0.01 level. This means the total cost is positively related to total output and the relation is significant at one per cent level of significance.

The relation of total cost (Y) as a function of total output (X), in the form of regression turns out to be as follows.

Y = -695135 + 10596.90 X**

SE (777.23)

t (13.638)

$R^2 = 0.85$ $F_{(1,88)} = 185.99^{**}$

The model is indicative of the fact that total cost is a positive function of total output in the college education and the relation is significant at one per cent level of significance. Both coefficient of determination and the analysis of variance for regression show that a major part of variation in dependent variable is explained by the independent variable. Thus the total cost as a function of total output of the system is behaving as expected. Going to disaggregate level by type of ownership yields the following results. Total cost is positively related both in case of government and private aided colleges and the regression model gives coefficient of determination higher than 60 per cent. But the relation is statistically week in case of private unaided colleges. This implies that every increase in strength is matched by an increase in the total cost in case of government and aided private colleges but it is not so in case of unaided colleges.

Table 5.18

Regression Results of Total Cost as a Function of Total Enrollment

Type of College	Constant	Coefficient	Standard Error	R^2	F Statistics
Govt.	2797544	9106.48	1154.08**	0.72	62.26**
Pvt. Aided	-1520248	11203.44	1346.72**	0.63	69.20**
Pvt. Unaided	1071393	3836.93	1527.07*	0.24	6.313*

* Significant at 0.02 level.

** Significant at 0.01 level.

To identify the underlying curve of the functional relationship of cost and output we have implemented nine different functional forms as shown in the Table 5.19. On the basis of analysis of variance of all regressions, it can be said that almost all the functional forms explain a good part of variation in the dependent variable. The value of coefficient of determination for different curves shows that the linear curve has the highest value (R^2=0.85). For further analysis, the linear curve can be used with a greater confidence for further regression analysis.

Hence, the two can be safely used to arrive at any measure of average or unit cost. The bahaviour of unit cost in college education has approximately a normal distribution with a slight positive skewness. This implies that there are a large number of colleges with higher than average unit cost.

Table 5.19

Curve Fitting Results for Total Cost as a Function of Total Output

Curve Type	R-Square	$F_{(2,87)}$
Linear	0.85	185.99**
Logarithmic	0.73	101.529**
Inverse	0.22	25.078**
Quadratic	0.68	91.976**
Cubic	0.69	64.339**
Compound	0.60	135.809**
Power	0.69	200.596**
S-Type	0.43	67.985**
Growth	0.61	135.810**
Exponential	0.61	134.711**

Source: Calculated

To find out the cost minimizing output of the system and the subsystems therein, the simple quadratic function as follows has been used: $Y = a + bX + cX^2$; where the Y is the total cost and X is the total output. The cost minimizing output has been computed for the entire sample as a whole and for the three types of colleges classified according to ownership. The model did not generate a viable solution in any case. It is primarily because of the fact that correlation between unit cost and the total enrolment is positive and very week. It is 0.041 and is statistically insignificant. This shows that the unit cost in college education is poorly related to enrolment of the system. It is primarily because of two reasons. First, the unit cost measure we have analyzed is basically a recurring cost component only and secondly, salaries are a major component of this recurring cost. Enrollment has proved to be a poor determinant of such a salary dominant unit recurring cost. Hence any further exercise to arrive at an optimum cost and following analysis thereof is not a viable proposition.

To conclude we can say, this kind of analysis of recurring unit cost should be considered with a caution because it does not depict the technological and allocation efficiencies. The output is quantity only and the aspect of quality has altogether been ignored. The unit cost is just indicative and not an optimum in any way.

III

RECURRING COST RECOVERY PATTERN

Percentage distribution of income (*Table 5.20*) from all sources for the sampled colleges shows that the system of college education is basically dependent on the grant-in-aid. This dependence is to the extent of 72.15 per cent of the total income. Major source of this grant-in-aid is the state government. Income from operations in colleges of Punjab is just 27.85 per cent. Tuition fee generates just 4.96 per cent of the total income and funds contribute 22.24 per cent of the total income. That is to say student contribution to the total income is to the tune of 27.20 per cent of the total income in college education.

Ownership category based analysis highlights the ground realities of the system. It shows 95.44 per cent of the total income of government colleges is formed by grant-in-aid only. This grant-in-aid figure is just 47.72 per cent in case of private aided colleges and is nil for the unaided private colleges. Tuition fee contributes just 0.70 per cent of the income and funds contribute 3.60 per cent of the income in case of government colleges. Income from operations is just 4.56 per cent of total income in case of government colleges. Private aided colleges are generating more than half (52.28%) of their income from operations. In case of private aided colleges 45.62 percentage of the total income is formed by funds and fee share is 5.43 per cent. Private unaided colleges are generating their entire income from operations. Fee share is 41.93 per cent and funds are

Table 5.20

Composition of Cost Recovery in College Education in Punjab

Type of College	Tuition Fee	Funds	Other Income	Total Income	Govt. Grant-in-Aid	Other Aid	Total Aid	Total Recovery
Ownership-wise								
Govt.	0.70	3.60	0.26	4.56	94.46	0.97	95.44	100.00
Pvt. Aided	5.43	45.62	1.22	52.28	46.45	1.28	47.72	100.00
Pvt. Unaided	41.93	57.30	0.77	100.00	0.00	0.00	0.00	100.00
Location-wise								
Urban	3.62	19.52	0.52	23.66	75.52	0.82	76.34	100.00
Semi-Urban	11.51	29.93	0.89	42.33	54.71	2.96	57.67	100.00
Rural	9.36	35.34	1.27	45.98	53.06	0.96	54.02	100.00
Size-wise								
Small	13.74	33.22	0.59	47.55	49.51	2.95	52.45	100.00
Medium	11.34	33.15	0.90	45.39	54.10	0.51	54.61	100.00
Big	2.63	18.73	0.59	21.95	77.15	0.89	78.05	100.00
All	4.96	22.24	0.64	27.85	71.13	1.02	72.15	100.00

Source: Calculated.

57.30 per cent of the total income. So in private aided colleges share of fee component is almost seven times and in private unaided this share is almost sixty times as compared to the same in case of government colleges. Private, both aided and unaided colleges are managing themselves by depending more on charging excessive funds from the students as tuition fee is fixed by the universities/ State.

Area-wise analysis shows that urban colleges get 76.34 per cent of their income in the form of grant-in-aid. This is just 57.67 per cent and 54.02 per cent for semi-urban and rural colleges respectively. Urban colleges of the state produce 23.66 per cent of the total income from operations. Income from operations is the highest in case rural colleges (47.55%). It is followed by semi-urban colleges (45.98%). Size-wise analysis of the institutions in the state shows that medium sized colleges get 78.05 per cent of the total income in the form of grant-in-aid. Big colleges get 72.15 per cent and small colleges get 54.61 per cent of the total income in the form of grant-in-aid. Same is the behaviour pattern of income from operations.

Thus the composition of income is indicative of the fact that government colleges are getting their almost entire income from grants and semi-government are getting less than half and private unaided are self-sustaining. Urban area, medium sized colleges are the major gainers and rural area and smaller institutions are relatively the losers in case of grant-in-aid. In terms of income from operations rural and small sized are sustaining on fees and funds and urban and medium sized are the gainers of present regime.

Tuition Fee and Funds

In the wake of privatization the institutions of higher education are expected to generate their own resources. Most of the higher education institutions have followed the way of enhancing the tuition fees and the funds chargeable from the students to raise the resources. Tuition fee per student is given in Table 5.21. Per student tuition fee in government colleges is Rs. 159; in private aided colleges it is Rs. 512 and in private unaided colleges it is Rs. 3162. Private unaided colleges are thus charging twenty times higher tuition fees as compared to government colleges and six times more as compared to private aided colleges. This wide variation is indicated by the analysis of variance also (F= 8.323).

Table 5.21

Distribution of Tuition Fee Charged in Colleges of Punjab

Type of College	Average Tuition Fee Charged (Rs.)	Coefficient of Variation (%)	F-Statistics
Ownership-wise			
Government	159	127.81	
Private Aided	512	96.27	
Private Unaided	3162	174.92	8.323**
Location-wise			
Urban	1321	311.28	
Semi-urban	976	174.70	
Rural	727	142.72	0.343
Size-wise			
Small	1741	274.16	
Medium	965	181.33	
Big	466	149.37	1.363
Total	**755**	**179.11**	–

** Significant at 1%.

Source: Primary Data.

Location-wise analysis of tuition fee per student underscores the fact that urban area colleges are charging slightly higher fee as compared to the other two categories. In urban area colleges tuition fee is Rs. 1,321; in semi-urban area colleges it is Rs. 976 and in rural area colleges it is Rs. 727. There is a wide variation within the colleges in the individual categories but the difference in tuition fees among the colleges of different locations is statistically insignificant (F= 0.343).

Likewise, tuition fee is higher in small sized colleges and lower in big sized colleges. There are wide variations within the three categories, but the variation is insignificant among the three categories (F= 1.363).

Higher education institutions, next to tuition fee, depend upon several kinds of funds from the students. A look on annual amount of funds per student (*Table 5.22*) shows that government colleges collect Rs. 813 per student as funds. On the other hand private aided colleges charge Rs. 3,420 and private unaided colleges charge Rs. 3,955 per year as funds. So private aided colleges are charging four times and private unaided colleges arc charging five times funds as compared to government colleges. There is a wide variation with in private aided colleges as far as fund charges are concerned. This is shown by relatively higher value of coefficient of variation. Location-wise analysis and size wise analysis of funds charged per student does not show statistically significant difference. Almost a similar behaviour pattern is there.

Recovery of Recurring Cost from Tuition Fee

Tuition fee as a percentage of total recurring cost is given in Table 5.23. In government colleges 1.50 per cent of total recurring cost is recovered from the fee charges. Private aided colleges recover 6.86 per cent of their total cost from tuition fee only and in private unaided colleges 55.40 per cent of the total recurring cost is recovered through tuition fee. Thus the private unaided colleges charge 37 times tuition fee as compared to government colleges and eight times as compared to private aided colleges. Location wise distribution of tuition fee as a percentage of total recurring cost does not show any significant difference. It varies within 16 to 18 per cent (F= 0.030). Another interesting fact about the tuition fee is highlighted by size-wise distribution of this data. In small sized colleges' tuition fee as a percentage of recurring cost is 22.46, in medium colleges it is 21.59 and in big sized colleges it is 7.47. Small and medium sized colleges are, therefore, recovering three times total recurring cost from tuition fee as compared to the big colleges.

Table 5.22

Distribution of Funds Charged in Colleges of Punjab

(Rs.)

Type of College	Average Funds Charged (Rs.)	Coefficient of Variation (%)	F-Statistics
Ownership-wise			
Government	813	58.59	
Private Aided	3420	88.58	
Private Unaided	3955	53.48	13.155**
Location-wise			
Urban	2549	104.24	
Semi-urban	2818	79.02	
Rural	3140	90.73	0.425
Size-wise			
Small	3566	81.43	
Medium	2785	89.05	
Big	2040	115.02	2.523
Total	**12271**	**94.41**	–

Source: Primary Data.

** Significant at 1%.

Majority of the colleges (N=46) are charging tuition fees up to five per cent of recurring cost (*Table 5.24*). In this category, most of the colleges are government colleges, followed by this there are 22 colleges which are charging tuition fees which is between 5-10 per cent of their recurring cost. There are certain notable exceptions also as there are five colleges which are recovering a very high percentage of their recurring cost as tuition fee. Among these colleges, there are generally private unaided colleges.

Table 5.23

Tuition Fee as a Percentage of Total Recurring Cost in Colleges of Punjab

Type of College	Tuition Fee as a percentage of Total Recurring Expenditure (%)	Coefficient of Variation (%)	F-Statistics
Ownership-wise			
Government	1.50	138.43	
Private Aided	6.86	161.08	
Private Unaided	55.40	136.33	14.309**
Location-wise			
Urban	18.37	306.76	
Semi-urban	15.99	158.16	
Rural	16.13	182.93	0.030
Size-wise			
Small	22.46	193.40	
Medium	21.59	269.76	
Big	7.47	257.18	1.089
Total	**16.62**	**247.11**	–

Source: Primary Data.

** Significant at 1%.

Surplus per Unit

In case of higher education surplus may be defined as the difference of total cost recovery and the total recurring cost. The analysis of surplus generated per student (*Table 5.25*) gives an indication about the economic health of an institution. Annual surplus generation per student is Rs. 6034.80 in government colleges and is only Rs. 717.18 in private unaided colleges. The private aided colleges have a deficit of Rs. 1,358 per student per year as far as the surplus generation is concerned. Most of the deficit generating institutions of higher education belong to semi-urban areas and are medium sized institutions. Majority of the surplus generating institutions are located in urban areas and are the bigger institutions in terms of student strength. The higher surplus generation of private unaided colleges is on the basis of cutting down some important heads of expenditure.

Table 5.24

Tuition Fee as a Percentage of Total Recurring Cost in Colleges of Punjab

Tuition Fee as a percentage of total recurring cost	Frequency
0 – 5	46
5 – 10	22
10 – 15	4
15 – 20	6
20 – 25	2
35 – 40	1
40 – 45	1
50 – 55	1
60 – 65	1
75 – 80	1
110 –320	5

Source: Calculated.

Table 5.25

Distribution of Surplus per Student in Colleges of Punjab

Type of College	Average Surplus (Rs.)	Coefficient of Variation	F-Statistics
Ownership-wise			
Government	6034.80	509.67	
Private Aided	-1358.09	-543.59	
Private Unaided	717.18	622.13	1.412
Location-wise			
Urban	2786.90	898.86	
Semi-urban	-279.29	-1446.30	
Rural	18.46	27311.00	0.290
Size-wise			
Small	855.83	708.51	
Medium	-229.50	-1607.30	
Big	3228.43	920.80	0.291
Total	**2137.17**	**1100.12**	–

Source: Primary Data.

IV

NON-RECURRING EXPENDITURE

Non-recurring cost, once for all cost, is a sort of capital expenditure. To get an idea about the nature and quantum of this expenditure, we have arrived at an average of last five years' expenditure under each non-recurring head. It is not a cost in economic sense; it is just a financial expenditure totally unrelated to life, efficiency and productivity. The distribution of components of non-recurring expenditure is given in Table 5.26. More than one-half of the non-recurring expenditure in the state goes for building and furniture only. It is 44.35 per cent for building and 7.13 per cent for furniture. Equipment expenditure share is 32.99 per cent and library expenditure

Table 5.26

Composition of Non-Recurring Expenditure in College Education in Punjab

(Per cent)

Type of College	Library Expenditure	Buildings Expenditure	Furniture Expenditure	Equipment Expenditure	Total Non-Recurring Expenditure
Ownership-wise					
Government	26.60	31.99	8.58	32.83	100.00
Pvt. Aided	13.85	47.76	6.54	31.85	100.00
Pvt. Unaided	11.99	42.12	8.13	37.76	100.00
Location-wise					
Urban	15.22	41.59	7.26	35.93	100.00
Semi-Urban	13.95	48.84	5.21	32.00	100.00
Rural	17.76	49.87	8.18	24.18	100.00
Size-wise					
Small	13.26	38.49	7.35	40.90	100.00
Medium	15.23	48.26	7.53	28.98	100.00
Big	16.18	44.52	6.95	32.35	100.00
All	15.53	44.35	7.13	32.99	100.00

Source: Calculated data.

is 15.53 per cent. Normally building and furniture cost is tied with the grants destined for this purpose. Whenever a grant is received, it is spent for these non-recurring heads of expenditure. Building component share is highest in case of private aided colleges (47.76%) followed by private unaided colleges (42.12%) and government colleges (31.99%). This is because most of the government colleges are old in the state, instead of new construction, it is the renovation/alteration of the building on which most of the non-recurring component is spent. Slightly higher building component in case of private colleges is because all such colleges have diversified into new and emerging area which needed extension or construction of building work. That is why in private colleges, along with building and equipment share is also slightly higher.

The share of building component is the highest in rural areas followed by semi-urban and urban areas in order. The share of equipment has behaved in a reverse manner. Equipment expenditure share is highest in urban areas followed by semi-urban and rural area colleges. Thus building construction has taken place in rural areas and equipment buying has been done in the urban areas. Percentage share of equipment expenditure is 40.90 per cent in small sized colleges as compared to 32.35 per cent in big colleges. This implies that small sized private unaided colleges are a new phenomenon in the state and government colleges are an age old system. The cut in aid has severely affected the library component. As against 26.60 per cent of total expenditure in government colleges, all other categories of institutions have spent in the range of 15 to 16 per cent only.

Library

Non recurring expenditure per student spent by an institution gives an idea about the quantity and quality of infrastructure provided by an institution. Total non recurring expenditure on library per student (Table 5.27) is the highest in private unaided colleges. It is followed by

Table 5.27

Distribution of Non-Recurring Expenditure on Library Per Student in College of Punjab

Type of College	Average Expenditure on Library (Rs.)	Coefficient of Variation (%)	F-Statistics
Ownership-wise			
Government	42.65	127.69	
Private Aided	57.35	73.10	
Private Unaided	66.45	105.86	1.184
Location-wise			
Urban	56.44	96.38	
Semi-urban	50.47	60.21	
Rural	56.50	113.54	0.081
Size-wise			
Small	69.50	106.45	
Medium	44.96	74.87	
Big	51.53	86.06	1.637

Source: Primary Data.

private aided and government colleges in order. It is Rs. 42.65 per student in case of government colleges; Rs. 57.35 in case of private aided colleges and Rs. 66.45 in case of private unaided colleges. Non-recurring expenditure per student is relatively lower in semi-urban area colleges as compared to colleges of urban or rural areas. Size wise analysis shows that small sized colleges spend more on library expenditure per unit as compared to the medium and big sized colleges.

Building

Building is generally a major component of non-recurring expenditure. Since most of the government colleges are old and very little new building is there. That is why the non-recurring building expenditure per student comes to be only Rs. 86.03 per student.

Table 5.28

Distribution of Non-Recurring Expenditure on Building Per Student in Colleges of Punjab

Type of College	Average Expenditure on Building (Rs.)	Coefficient of Variation	F-Statistics
Ownership-wise			
Government	86.03	338.30	
Private Aided	222.26	101.92	
Private Unaided	126.13	142.28	2.835
Location-wise			
Urban	154.88	124.76	
Semi-urban	137.29	110.33	
Rural	178.43	188.15	0.162
Size-wise			
Small	170.66	193.10	
Medium	139.60	108.84	
Big	168.56	130.48	0.143
Total	**169.21**	**132.33**	–

Source: Primary Data.

On the other hand, private colleges are expanding their operations by introducing new job-oriented courses in the field of management, technology and computer application. This required a heavy investment on construction, repair or renovation of existing building. Private aided colleges are spending on an average Rs. 222.26 per student and private unaided colleges are spending Rs.126.13 on building per student. Majority of the new courses are being run in urban colleges but the figure of building expenditure per student is high in rural colleges. This is because of the fact that most of the private aided colleges situated in rural areas have gone in for new construction or renovation of existing building for new courses. Size-wise distribution of non-recurring expenditure per student displays a mixed trend. Medium sized colleges have spent relatively less amount per unit on building as compared to the other two categories.

Furniture

The annual furniture expenditure per student is the lowest in government colleges and is the highest in private unaided colleges (Table 5.29). It is because of the fact that most of the private unaided colleges falling in this case are new colleges and they have spent almost three times on this head as compared to the government colleges. Further the higher furniture expenditure per student is associated with urban area colleges and the colleges of smaller size in terms of student strength.

Table 5.29

Distribution of Non-Recurring Expenditure on Furniture Per Student in Colleges of Punjab

Type of College	Average Expenditure on Furniture (Rs.)	Coefficient of Variation (%)	F-Statistics
Ownership-wise			
Government	13.03	251.06	
Private Aided	31.88	92.21	
Private Unaided	41.31	231.18	1.909
Location-wise			
Urban	35.74	186.07	
Semi-urban	16.82	109.17	
Rural	25.46	151.00	0.877
Size-wise			
Small	37.43	211.86	
Medium	22.40	113.53	
Big	26.40	126.44	0.655
Total	**26.93**	**127.33**	–

Source: Primary Data.

Equipment

Equipment is the next component of non-recurring cost. It generally includes office equipment, laboratory equipment, and computer equipment. Equipment expenditure is Rs. 32.92 per student per year in government colleges, Rs.148.83 in private unaided colleges and Rs.257.40 in private unaided colleges (*Table 5.30*).

Table 5.30

Distribution of Non-Recurring Expenditure on Equipment Per Student in Colleges of Punjab

Type of College	Average Expenditure on Equipment (Rs.)	Coefficient of Variation (%)	F-Statistics
Ownership-wise			
Government	32.92	201.97	
Private Aided	148.83	129.19	
Private Unaided	257.40	339.26	1.425
Location-wise			
Urban	198.81	323.14	
Semi-urban	103.94	147.32	
Rural	81.80	177.44	0.630
Size-wise			
Small	231.80	329.04	
Medium	83.90	118.31	
Big	109.96	159.93	0.871
Total	**119.96**	**162.23**	–

Source: Primary Data.

So on equipment, private unaided colleges spend eight times as compared to government colleges and private aided colleges spend five times as compared to government colleges. Larger share of equipment expenditure per student is distributed in favour of urban area colleges and the rural area colleges are deprived ones. The size-wise distribution of non-recurring equipment expenditure per student shows an interesting dichotomy. Small sized colleges have spent very high amounts, to the tune of Rs. 231.80 per student on equipment because of their compulsion to start new courses and the big colleges have spent a slightly lower amount of Rs. 119.96 per student as equipment because of availability of surplus.

Composition of Non-recurring Funds

Since, historically, the major components of non-recurring component of the expenditure have been funded by the government agencies. Present position of non-recurring expenditure (*Table 5.31*) in the State shows that government funding of the non-recurring is just 27.66 per cent and rest of the balance comes from other sources. Government colleges in the State have get 57.36 per cent of their non-recurring expenditure from the government agencies. In the private aided colleges, the figure for government support is just 23.75 per cent and in private unaided category colleges, it is just 16.18 per cent. Other than the government agencies, the non-recurring

Table 5.31

Composition of Non-Recurring Funds in Colleges of Punjab

College Type	Government Grant-in-Aid	Others Grants	Total Aid
Ownership-wise			
Government	57.36	42.64	100.00
Private Aided	23.75	76.25	100.00
Private Unaided	16.18	83.82	100.00
Location-wise			
Urban	26.68	73.32	100.00
Semi-Urban	13.25	86.75	100.00
Rural	40.92	59.08	100.00
Size-wise			
Small	46.83	53.17	100.00
Medium	40.51	59.49	100.00
Big	12.53	87.47	100.00
All	27.66	72.34	100.00

Source: Calculated.

component comes from own funds generated from operations or collected from other agencies. The share of government aid for non-recurring has been 26.68 per cent, 13.25 per cent and 40.92 per cent for urban, semi-urban or rural area colleges. In terms of size, small and medium sized colleges have got 46.83 per cent and 40.50 per cent respectively. The non-recurring component from government and the big sized colleges' dependence on this component is just 12.53 per cent. Thus the asset generation process is dependent the capacity to generate income from operations. Private unaided and the big sized institutions manage the non recurring expenditure at their own, and the government institutions or the institutions in rural areas have to depend on the government agencies.

Pattern of Non-recurring Expenditure and Recovery

Future sustainability of a system depends on its capacity to generate the surplus per unit of output. In the education system surplus is generally defined as the difference of income and the expenditure. In terms of non-recurring expenditure recovery the system of college education is basically a deficit and not a surplus generating (*Table 5.32*). Over the sampled colleges range, more than Rs. 27,000 per student is the deficit each year. The government colleges have this deficit figure at Rs. 10,362 per student; the private aided colleges stand at the mark of Rs. 33,864 per student; and the unaided colleges have Rs. 45,782 per student per year. Area wise, the urban, semi-urban and the rural institutions depict a range of Rs. 24,000 to 32,000 per student. Small colleges have the largest deficit per student and the medium colleges have the smallest deficit. Thus the unaided, rural or the small sized institutions are spending more on non recurring components than actually they receive for this purpose. Such an over expenditure, if properly and strategically planned, strengthens the institution in future. But if it is unplanned business proposal, can prove to be a serious drag on the source of funds of the system.

Table 5.32

Pattern of Non-Recurring Expenditure Recovery in Colleges in Punjab

(Rs.)

Type of College	Recovery	Expenditure	Surplus	Surplus/Unit
Ownership-wise				
Government	1439400	5081073	-3641673	-10362
Private Aided	3359842	21967455	-18607613	-33864
Private Unaided	270200	5443472	-5173272	-45782
Location-wise				
Urban	2607685	21076904	-18469612	-26686
Semi-Urban	498000	4954515	-4456515	-31954
Rural	1963757	6460582	-4496825	-24661
Size-wise				
Small	1660437	5076118	-3415681	-32401
Medium	2254120	6697958	-4443838	-19785
Big	11548885	20717924	-19563039	-28606
All	5069442	32492000	-27422558	-27046

Source: Calculated.

Conclusion

Thus to sum up, we can say that the structure of cost and cost recovery in college education in Punjab does not reflect a model characterized by long-term strategy and vision. It is biased in favour of urban area. Government withdrawal from college education, on the name of privatization, has made the system to be short-run profit motivated. Human capital and its highest form the intellectual capital development has lost the ground. This is high time for state government to come up with a vision on higher education and make it more inclusive.

Conclusions and Policy Implications

Resources are often in short supply and there is an urgent need to maximize the efficiency of inputs in the education sector and thereby eliminate the wastage of precious resources. Various commissions have emphasized to obtain maximum possible output from a given level of investment. Education sector is faced with the challenge of raising effectiveness of utilization of available resources. The efficient management of higher education concerns not only with measures to reduce recurring costs but also with the recovery of these costs. Subsidized for decades together and nurtured in a planned economy and public sector kind of environment, like other sectors, education sector has never been prepared for a market oriented approach. The market guided system requires a maximization of revenue and minimization of the cost. It is in this context that the economic analysis of cost and the cost recovery in college education is the need of the hour. The study is an attempt to analyze cost and cost recovery of college education in Punjab by going to a disaggregate level.

The main objectives of the study are:

(a) to study the structure of higher education in Punjab;

(b) to analyze the recurring cost and its components;

(c) to study the effect of ownership, location and size of institution on recurring cost and its components;

(d) to evaluate the recurring cost recovery and surplus generation mechanism; and

(e) to make the policy recommendations for effective educational planning and administration.

For economic analysis of cost, universe of the study is composed of 206 colleges. For drawing a sample, stratified random sampling technique has been used. The sample size of the study is more than forty percent of the universe. For drawing the sample, the universe has been divided into three strata: government colleges, government aided private colleges; and unaided colleges. Out of the universe, sample drawn is composed of 26 government colleges, 42 private aided colleges and 22 unaided colleges. Thus the total sample size of the study is of 90 colleges. Using a well structured questionnaire, through personal interview method, primary data has been collected. Typically, an institution incurs two types of costs: recurring and non-recurring cost. Due to inherent problems in the measurement of non-recurring cost, much of the work deals with the analysis of recurring cost, its components and recovery patterns. In a passing reference, non-recurring expenditure has also been analyzed but the prime focus of the study is on recurring cost only. Student enrolment has been used as an output for analysis of unit cost of education. The work has used the tabular technique along with appropriate statistical techniques.

Conclusions

Education commands pivotal place in socio-economic development, it is the single largest contributor to economic growth. The spread of education both in the quantitative and qualitative spectrum entails tremendous growth potential by providing big push to the human capabilities. An appropriate education system cultivates knowledge, skill, positive attitude, awareness and sense of responsibility towards rights and duties and imparts inner strength to face oppression, humiliation and inequality. In the light of the objectives and the methodology outlined above, following are the broad conclusions that emerge from the analysis:

1. The general socio-economic scenario in the State of Punjab exhibits complex relationship between economic growth and social sector development. Punjab State has been experiencing serious imbalance in terms of high income levels and laggard quality of human resources. The reasonably high level of state income co-exists with relatively moderate level of human resources when the latter have been measured in terms of educational and health standards. There is inadequate transfer of resources towards the improvement of the quality of human resources.

2. A person who is able to read and write with understanding in any language is recorded as literate. In Punjab, during the last decades literacy rate has been rising. As against 33.67 per cent in the year 1971, it has reached the level of 70 per cent in 2001. Gender-wise breakup of the literacy indicates that in the year 2001, female literacy stands at 63.55 per cent as against the same for male at 75.63 per cent. Low female literacy in Punjab is really a matter of concern for the planners and academicians.

3. Over a period of time the situation is improving. Punjab has fared well in reducing the gap between male and female literacy, which decreased from 15.25 per cent in 1991 to 12.08 per cent in 2001. There is also a noticeable change between urban and rural literacy. The gap has significantly narrowed down in the last

decade according to Census 2001. The gap between urban and rural literacy has reduced from 19.31 per cent point in 1991 to 13.97 per cent points in 2001. But in spite of these positive trends, there are still 94.35 lakh illiterates in the State. It is a matter of great concern that in spite of having improved its literacy rate figure, the rank of Punjab has slide down from the 12th position in 1971 to the 16th in 2001, when compared to other States and UTs in India. At present, Kerala has the highest literacy rate of 90.92 per cent while Bihar has the lowest of 47.53 per cent.

4. As far as the university education segment is concerned, the number of institutions has grown very fast in the State but the number of teachers has not grown in synchronization of it. In the multi-faculty colleges the teacher strength has grown with the number of institutions. Same is the case with engineering and medical education. But in teacher training colleges, where teacher only is the basic input, the number of teachers has not grown in consonance with the number of institutions.

5. The higher education system of the State, initially a state planned and financed, has been thrown open to the private sector in the decade nineties. The government has started withdrawing from financing higher education and the higher education institutions are expected to be self-sustaining. As a result of this, there has been a drastic structural change in the higher education system of the State. Traditional multi-faculty arts, science, commerce and home science colleges have introduced many self financed job oriented courses. Universities of the state, basically perceived centers of higher learning and research have also entered into the business of college education.

6. Another dimension of this structural change in education is that enhancing existing fee or charging

exorbitant fees is a common phenomenon. In the name of sponsored seats, less qualified students replace the qualified intake of the institutions. The higher education in the State is characterized by the feature of exclusion of rural and the poor. Resource mobilization, that too just a short-term, is the only objective. Long-term business of an institution is a function of its brand-image and a short-term business is to sell whatever has a market. Higher education system of the state has moved somewhat on the second option.

7. In a growing and leading State like Punjab, where thorough structural transformation of existing structure is need of the time; the research and development should have been on the top of the agenda. The number of students going in for research courses is negligible. It is less than even one per cent of the students who started their primary education years back. The number of female students is above the half mark. Number of scheduled caste students in Ph.D. research that was 1.35 per cent in 1990 has touched the zero mark. In M.Phil. programme, historically the number of scheduled caste students has never crossed the seven per cent mark. This is primarily because of the higher cost and the long duration of such programmes.

8. Major chunk of students in post graduate education in the state is in courses of arts, science and commerce. Number of students in post graduation in engineering, medical and management education is very small. As compared to Commerce, the number of students in science is almost double of it and number of students in arts is more than ten times of it. In the temporal dimension, as compared to the early seventies, there is a three-fold increase in the number of arts students. On the other hand, in the last few decades there has

been more than ten times rise in number of M.Sc. students. Number of post-graduate course students with commerce is also consistently improving. So in the past, as compared to arts courses, the student strength has significantly improved in the science and commerce courses, but still the number of students in post graduation in arts is on the higher side.

9. The percentage of female students in post-graduate courses in arts, science and commerce initially that was below forty per cent in the decade of seventies, crossed half mark in early eighties and has crossed 60 per cent mark in the decade of nineties. The percentage of female students individually in the three streams is showing a tendency to cross the three-fourth mark shortly, but in case of scheduled caste category, the number of students availing reservation is still higher for males as compared to females.

10. Graduate courses are the feeding area for post graduate courses. A look on absolute numbers shows that all the three streams are popular. Students are oddly distributed among the three streams, with a highest number of students in arts followed by science and commerce in order. Currently the percentage of scheduled caste students in graduate courses is below twelve per cent. The situation is worst in commerce and science graduate courses. More of the male are availing the reservation than the female.

11. As compared to graduate courses, the state shows that the per centage of female students in total has increased in all streams of post graduation. In arts, it rose from 62 per cent to 71 per cent and in commerce it rose from 46 per cent to 82 per cent, as soon as there is shift from graduation to post graduation. The reason behind this drastic change is that all the three traditional streams are not job oriented. Male students

in the state have a mindset of doing at least graduation and then shifting to newly started job oriented courses in administration, management, computers and law and female stick to traditional higher education to reach the research level.

12. Professional courses related to engineering, technology, medical and education are relatively new phenomena in the state. The number of engineering and technology students, which used to be less than 2000 till early nineties, has crossed the 17,000 mark. Right from the decade of 1970s till date, the number of students in medical courses has grown to near 2760 in 2004 as against 2088 in 1970. The number of B.Ed. students has increased a lot. As such the professional courses are becoming equally popular among the female students.

13. Most of the unaided colleges of the state are relatively small colleges. Further, the strength-wise big colleges are in the urban area; medium colleges are in the semi-urban area and the small colleges are in the rural area. The study clearly indicates that the aided college education, both government and privately owned in the state is heavily biased in the favour of urban area.

14. Multi-faculty colleges are still operating in a traditional set up of humanities followed by science, commerce and other professional courses in order of strength. In terms of student strength, the much talked about computer and management courses are just six per cent. Both government and private aided colleges have experimented new courses for cost recovery within traditional framework of retaining arts, science and commerce courses. But the unaided have skipped science and commerce courses and have directly jumped from arts to the professional courses. Most of the professional courses have been set up in the urban area colleges and that too by the big sized colleges. Thus urban area,

along with large size and aid from the government has played a major role in growth and diversification college education.

15. Private unaided colleges have on an average 20 teachers per college and government colleges and private aided colleges have almost double of this strength. There is a slight difference between government colleges and aided colleges as far as the teaching staff strength is concerned. Average teaching staff strength in urban colleges is double of rural area colleges and one half times of semi-urban area colleges. So the rural area colleges are in a disadvantaged situation as far as number of teachers per institution is concerned.

16. In terms of nature of employment majority of the teachers working on permanent basis are in government colleges. The private aided and private unaided colleges are depending on teaching staff recruited on temporary or ad hoc basis. Further, most of this temporary and ad hoc staff is associated with colleges of semi-urban or rural area colleges. Size of the colleges does not affect this distribution.

17. Salary component forms a major chunk of recurring cost. On the whole 92.97 per cent of the total recurring cost goes to the salaries alone. In the present phase of competition, tight budget position of colleges in the State of Punjab leaves no space for expenditure on some of the important heads of inputs like library, furniture and building maintenance, equipment maintenance, consumables, extra-curricular activities and financial support to the needy and deserving ones.

18. Private unaided staff, both teaching and non-teaching is ill paid in comparison to the other two. Further, the higher salary share colleges are mostly the urban area colleges. The private institutions of the state manage their salary budget by keeping a check on number of

non-teaching employees and paying less to them. Thus the movement from government to aided private and then to private unaided leads to a continuous slide down in salary.

19. Next component of salary is the allowances, dearness allowance being the major allowance. Average amount of allowances per teacher in government colleges is double of private aided colleges' and triple of private unaided colleges. Privatization of higher education in Punjab has lead to a sharp cut in the allowances being paid to the teaching staff. Location-wise and size-wise differentials in allowances are pronounced because of skewed strength of employees in the institutions.

20. Pressure on salaries leaves no space for maintenance or other beyond the curriculum activities. In college education, the big infrastructure created in the past is getting deteriorated or becoming unserviceable only because of lack of availability of funds for repair and maintenance. Some of the renowned institutions in sports, free-ships and extra-curricular activities have gone into total fade-out due to lack of funds. The pressure on the funds has left the college education system to mean only the lecture delivery system and nothing more than this.

21. Total recurring cost per student is a best measure of average cost. Total recurring cost per student in government colleges is Rs. 12,413. It is Rs. 10,000 in case of aided and Rs. 6,453 in unaided colleges. So the government colleges are spending almost double and private aided are spending almost one and a half times as compared to the unaided colleges in the state. Hence, the private, medium sized and Semi-urban category colleges are operating at a relative lower recurring cost per unit. As per economic logic total output is a prime determinant of the cost and revenue

of a unit. The average cost of education in Punjab, has just crossed the minimum cost level. But, this cost efficiency, should not be taken to mean the operational or technical efficiency of the system.

22. The college education is basically dependent on the grant-in-aid from government. This dependence is to the extent of 72.15 per cent of the total income and income from operations in colleges of Punjab is just 27.85 per cent. Tuition fee generates just 4.96 per cent of the total income end funds contributes 22.24 per cent of the total income. That is to say student contribution to the total income is to the tune of 27.20 per cent of the total income in college education.

23. Ownership-wise grant-in-aid share in total income is 95.44 per cent in government colleges, 47.72 per cent in case of private aided colleges, and nil for the unaided private colleges. In private aided colleges, share of fee component is almost seven times and in private unaided this share is almost 60 times of the same in case of government colleges. Private, both aided and unaided colleges are managing themselves by charging excessive funds from the students, as fee is fixed by the universities/State. Thus, the composition of income is indicative of the fact that government colleges are getting their almost entire income from grants and semi-government are getting less than half and private unaided are self-financing.

24. Future sustainability of a system depends on its capacity to generate the surplus per unit of output. In the education system surplus is generally defined as the difference of income and the cost. The surplus is generated only in government and private unaided colleges. The private aided colleges suffer from deficits. Most of the deficit generating institutions of higher education belong to semi-urban areas and are medium sized institutions.

25. As a measure of cost recovery, generally, the tuition fee as a percentage of total recurring cost is used. Tuition fee as a percentage of total recurring cost is 1.50 per cent in government colleges. It is 6.86 per cent in private aided colleges and 55.40 per cent in case of private unaided colleges. Thus as a result of privatization, the tuition fee has become a main source of recovery.

26. At a point of time, non-recurring expenditure per student spent by an institution gives an idea about the quantity and quality of infrastructure provided by an institution. Present position of non-recurring expenditure in the state shows that government funding of the non-recurring is just 27.66 and rest of the balance comes from other sources. Government colleges in the state have got 57.36 per cent of their non-recurring expenditure from the government agencies. In the private aided colleges, the figure for government support is just 23.75 per cent and in private unaided category colleges, it is just 16.18 per cent. Other than the government agencies, the non-recurring component comes from own funds generated from operations or collected from other agencies. This option has been used by the private unaided and the big sized institutions.

Policy Implications

On the basis of above conclusions, following are the policy implications:

1. Presently, every current wave of market demand is serving as the only guide mark for investment. For example, millennium opening, characterized by information technology boom all around, led to mushrooming of information technology institutions. Many new institutions opened up and some of the existing ones replaced their traditional courses with new ones. Currently, teacher training education led boom,

is on the same lines. This impulsive response of the education system to short market demand surge leads to a massive mis-planned human resource orientation. The State of Punjab must prepare a strategic long term plan and a vision for higher education.

2. The emerging service sector in general and the knowledge economy in particular, need education to be developed as a system and that too in a targeted way. This needs to inculcate the feature of relevance and competencies in the college education. College education system must be synchronized with the job-oriented post-graduate courses so that the required competencies could be generated at the college level.

3. The study clearly indicates that the college education is heavily biased in the favour of urban area. The model of higher education has continuously excluded the rural and the poor. There is an urgent need of the time to make the current higher education system to be more inclusive in terms of price and space. This needs a centralized planning and administration of higher education in the State.

4. Teacher is basic input into the education system. Presently, a large section of the college education is being run by teachers recruited on adhoc or temporary basis. This adhocism must be replaced by a planned, perpetual, sustainable and viable system of recruitment, training and follow up. Private hands can not; it is the State only that can ensure such a system.

5. The tight budget position of colleges in the state leaves no space for expenditure on some of the important heads of inputs like library, furniture and building maintenance, equipment maintenance, consumables, extra-curricular activities and financial support to the needy and deserving ones. A viable mechanism of grant-in-aid should be created. It can be public, private or a collaborative one.

Thus, to sum up, we can say that the structure of cost and cost recovery in college education in Punjab does not reflect a model characterized by long-term strategy and vision. It is biased in favour of urban area. Government withdrawal from college education, on the name of privatization, has made the system to be short-run profit motivated. Human capital and its highest form the intellectual capital development has lost the ground. This is high time for state government to come up with a vision on higher education and make it more inclusive.

Bibliography

Agarwal, Raj (2002), "Globalization of Higher Education and WTO", *University News*, Vol. 40, No. 34, pp. 1-9.

Agarwal, V. and Sharma, U. R. (2002), "Privatization of Higher Education: Controversies and Suggestions", *University News*, Vol. 40, No. 49, pp. 1-4.

Ahmad, Nabi and Siddiqui, M.A. (2003), "Privatization of Higher Education: An Appraisal", *University News*, Vol. 41, No. 07, pp. 4-7.

Anderson, Arnold C. (1972), "Organizing Indian Educational Statistics for Action", *Economic and Political Weekly*, Nov. 4, 1972, pp. 2250-52.

Ansari, M.M. (1994), "Strategy of Funding Higher Education: Areas and Directions for Reforms", *Journal of Education Planning and Administration*, Vol. VIII, No. 1, pp. 87-101.

Azad, J.L. (1994), "Researches in Educational Finance: Past, Present and Future", *Journal of Higher Education*, Vol. 17, No. 3, pp. 371-379.

Azad, J.L. (1995), "Financing of Higher Education in India: With Special Reference to Resource Mobilization", *Journal of Higher Education*, Vol. 18, No. 4, pp. 643-656.

Bellew, Rosemary and Joseph De Stefano, (1991), *Costs and Finance of Higher Education in Pakistan*, The World Bank Report.

Brar, J.S. (1999), *Punjab's Educational Progress, and Educational Expenditure (1967-68 to 1993-94)*, Punjabi University, Patiala.

Chalam, K.S., (1978), "Expenditure on University Education: A Unit Cost Analysis", *Journal of Higher Education*, Vol. 4, No. 2, pp. 201-224.

Chalam, K.S. (2002), "Globalization of Education and Indigenization of Knowledge", *University News*, Vol. 40, No. 16, pp. 1-3.

Chalam, K.S. (2003), "The Changing Scenario of Higher Education: Coping with the Challenges in the Twenty-first Century, *University News*, Vol. 41, No. 28, pp. 1-4.

Chauhan, C.P.S. (2000), "Higher Education in India: Challenges of Global Trends", *University News*, Vol. 40, No. 17, July 1-7, pp. 4-9.

Dandekar, V.M. (1991): "Reform of Higher Education", *Economic and Political Weekly*, Nov. 16, pp. 2631-2637.

Dasgupta, R.K. (2000), "Education: Retrospect and Prospect", *Yojana*, May 2000.

Desai, A.S. (1992), "Impact of Monetary Crisis in Higher Education", *Journal of Higher Education*, Vol. 16, No. 1, pp. 118-120.

Desai, A.S. (1995), "Policies for Higher Education in India", *Journal of Higher Education*, Vol. 18, No. 4, pp. 667-686.

Deshpande, H.V. (2003), "Quality and Administration of Higher Education under Globalization: Challenges and Remedies", *University News*, Vol. 41, No. 10, pp. 3-5.

Dhesi, A.S. (1998), "Education: Incentive Structure, Misallocation of Resources and Policy Responses", *University News*, Vol. 36, No. 24, pp. 37-41.

Drysdale, R., (1985), *China: Management and Finance of Higher Education*, A World Bank Country Study.

Dutt, Ruddar, (1995), "Financing of Higher Education: Approaches and Priorities", *Journal of Higher Education*, Vol. 18 No. 1, pp. 63-81.

Dutt, Ruddar, "Unit Cost of Education — A Case Study of Haryana Colleges", *Asian Economic Review*, pp. 66-80.

El-Hout, M. Sabry, "Mobilizing Additional Financial Resources for Higher Education in Egypt", *Journal of Higher Education*, Vol. 1, No. 3 and 4, pp. 257-311.

Gill, Sucha Singh, et al. (2005), "Educational Development, Public Expenditure and Financing of Secondary Education in Punjab", *Journal of Educational Planning and Administration*, Vol. XIX, No. 3, pp. 335-374.

Ghuman, R. S. (1990), "Private Cost in Distance and Conventional Education in India", *Journal of Indian Education*, Vol. 15, No. 5, pp. 40-47.

Goel, B.P. (1985), "Private Cost of Post-Graduate Education.", *Journal of Indian Education*, Vol. 11, No. 2, pp. 58-63.

Goel, Chhaya and Goel, D.R. (2002), "Relationship of Higher Education", *University News*, Vol. 40, No. 26, pp. 1-4.

Hajela, P.D. (1996), "Education As a Toll for Social Uplift", *Yojana*, pp. 33-35.

Hinchliffe (1987), "Diversified Sources of Educational Finance — Lessons from Federalism", *Journal of Higher Education*, Vol. 1, No. 3 and 4, July and October.

Israney, S.M., (1996), "Higher Education: Global Trends and Lessons": In Devendra Thakur and D.N. Thakur (eds), *Studies in Educational Development* Vol. 3 – *Higher Education and Employment*, Deep and Deep Publications, New Delhi, pp. 53-57.

Iyer, V.R. (2004), "Higher Education in a Liberalized Economy", *University News*, Vol. 42, No. 01, January 05-11, pp. 7-13.

Jayaram, N. (1990), "Higher Education: State Policy and Social Constraints", *Journal of Higher Education*, Vol. 15, 1989-90.

Jena, S.L. (1980), "Cost-Quality Relation in Education", *Journal of Indian Education*, Vol. VI, No. 4, November, pp. 8-12.

Joseph, Thomas (2002), "Higher Education: An Investment for Empowerment", *University News*, Vol. 40, No. 44, pp. 1-4.

Joseph, Thomas (2003), "Higher Education: Changing Perspectives of the World Bank and the Lessons for India", *University News*, Vol. 41, No. 18, pp. 1-18.

Joshi, J.P. (2003), "Globalization: A Need for Change in Educational Management system", *University News*, Vol. 41, No. 20, pp. 7-13.

Kamat, A.R. (1967) "Unit Institutional Cost in Higher Education", *Artha Vijnana*, Vol. 1, No. 1, March, pp. 92-104.

Kamat, A.R. (1967), "Unit Institutional Cost in Higher Education – A Study in Method", *Artha Vijnana*, Vol. 9 No. 1, March, pp. 92-104.

Khan, Q.U., (1996), "Higher Education in India- Some Issues". In: Devendra Thakur and D.N. Thakur (eds), *Studies in Educational Development* Vol. 3- *Higher Education and Employment*, Deep and Deep Publications, New Delhi, pp. 70-90.

Kothari, V.N., (1966), "Factor Cost of Education in India", *The Indian Economic Journal*, Vol. XIII, No. 5, April-June, pp. 631-646.

Kshatriya, D. and Varsha P., (2003), "Contemporary Issues of Higher Education", *University News*, Vol. 41, No. 31, pp. 1-11.

Kurup, M.R. (2002), "General Higher Education: Time for a Rethinking", *University News*, Vol. 40, No. 6, pp. 1-6.

Lyer, V.R. (2004), "Higher Education in a Liberalized Economy", *University News*, Vol. 42, No. 1, pp. 7-13.

Majumdar (1987), "The Role of the Finance Commission-Planning in the Non-Plan Outlays in Higher Education", *Journal of Higher Education*, Vol. 1, No. 3 and 4, July and October, pp. 1-11.

Mathew, E.T. (1991), "Financial Aspects of Privatization of Higher Education", *Economic and Political Weekly*, pp. 866-869.

Mehta, B.C. (1993), "Financing of Higher Education", *Journal of Educational Planning and Administration*, Vol. VII, No. 1, pp. 63-74

Mingat and G. Jee Peng (1971), Education in Asia—A Comparative Study.

Misra, Baidyanath (2002), "Prospects of Restructuring of Higher Education", *University News*, Vol. 40, No. 2, pp. 1-6.

Mittar, Vishwa, et al., (2002), *Changing Structure of Education in Punjab: Some Issues and Policy Recommendations*, Punjabi University, Patiala.

Mohan, M.C. (1993), "Investment Criteria and Financing Education for Economic Development", *Journal of Educational Planning and Administration*, Vol. VII, No. 2, pp. 153-164.

Padmanabhan, C.B. (1971), "Cost Analysis in Educational Administration", *Yojana*, Nov. 28, pp. 11-12.

Paliwal, Dinesh K. (2002), "Globalization of India Education", *University News*, Vol. 40, No. 39, pp. 9-15.

Panda, G.S. and P.P. Padhi (1990), "Cost Effectiveness in Higher Education – A Case Study", *Journal of Educational Planning and Administration*, Vol. 4, No. 4, Oct. 1990, pp. 71-75.

Pandey, Asha (1987), "Problems in Indian Higher Education: Challenges and Counter Steps", *Journal of Indian Education*, Vol. 13, pp. 49-51.

Pandit, H.N. (1969), *Measurement of Cost Productivity and Efficiency of Education*, National Council of Educational Research and Training.

Parhar, Madhu (2002), "Enrollment Projection in Higher Education", *University News*, Vol. 40, No. 27, July 8-14, pp. 1-4.

Parkash, Shri (1996), *Cost of Education – Theoretical Explorations and Empirical Prognostication,* Anamika Publishers, New Delhi.

Parkash, Shri and Romesh Kumar Bansal (1985), *Unit Cost of College Education in Punjab*, Punjabi University, Patiala.

Patil, L.A. (2002), "Higher Education: Challenges, Excellence and Future", *University News*, Vol. 40, No. 27, pp. 12-17.

Patil, V.K., Sharma, P.N. and others (2002), "Education in the Context of the Changing World, *University News*, Vol. 40, No. 17, pp. 1-9.

Paul, Samuel (1970), "Management in Education: Social Costs and Returns", *Economic and Political Weekly*, May, pp.

Pillai, Latha and Ponmudiraj, B.S., (2002), "2002: The Year of Quality in Higher Education", *University News*, Vol. 40, No. 31, pp. 1-2.

Pillai, Neena (2003), "Restructuring the State Run Educational Institutions", *University News*, Vol. 41, No. 07, pp. 17-23.

Powar, K.B. (2002), WTO, GATS and Higher Education: An Indian Perspective, *University News*, Vol. 40, No. 23, pp. 10-16.

Prasad, M.S.V. *et al.* (2003), "Higher Education 2010: Pointers, Possibilities, Pitfalls and Principles", *University News*, Vol. 41, No. 49, pp. 7-15.

Psacharopoulos, Jee Peng Tan, Emannel Jimenez (1987), "Financing Education in Developing Countries: An Exploration of Policy Options", *Journal of Higher Education*, Vol. 1, No. 3 and 4, July and October.

Punelekar, S.P (1998), "Education, Polarization and Market — An Uneasy Relationship", *Man and Development*, Vol. XX, No. 3, September, pp. 22-35.

Raikhy, P.S., (December, 2003), *Unit Cost of Higher Education: A Study of Guru Nanak Dev University*, Amritsar.

Rajaiah, B. (1987): *Economics of Education*, Mittal Publications, Delhi.

Ramalingaswamy, Prabha (1986) "Methodological issues in an Estimation of the cost of Medical Education in India", *Journal of Social and Economic Studies*, Nos. 3, 4, pp. 359-367.

Ramdas, M., (1984), "Public Expenditure on Education — A Cost Benefit Study", *Journal of Higher Education*, Vol. X, No. 1, pp. 1-12.

Reddy, A. Ranga (2004), "Higher Education Needs Speedy Reforms", *University News*, Vol. 42, No. 17, pp. 5-10.

Roy, Allen, *et al.*, (2000), "Educational Expenditure of Large States- A Normative View", *Economic and Political Weekly*, Vol. XXXV, No. 17, April 22, pp. 1465-1469.

Sahoo, P.K., (1990), "Private Costs of Post Graduate Students of Himachal Pradesh University", *Journal of Education Planning and Administration*, Vol. 4, No. 3, pp. 49-57.

Saleem, Shaikh (2003), "Privatization of Higher Education", *University News*, Vol. 41, No. 28, July 14-20, pp. 5-7.

Salim, A. Abdul (1995), "Subsidization of Higher Education in Kerala: A Socio-Economic Analysis", *Indian Economic Journal*, Vol. 42, No. 4, April-June, pp. 97-110.

Salim, A. Abdul (1996), "Institutional Cost of Higher Education — A Case Study of Kerala", *Manpower Journal,* Vol. XXXII, No. 1, April, pp. 1-14.

Shah, A.B. (1967), "Higher Education: Problems of Expansion", in A.B.Shah (ed.) *Higher Education in India*, Lalvani Publishing House, Bombay, pp. 1-9.

Shariff, A. and Ghosh, P.K. (2000), "Indian Education Scene and the Public Gap", *Economic and Political Weekly*, Vol. XXXV, No. 16, April 15, pp. 1396-1406.

Sharma, Madan Mohan (1992), *Financial Management of Universities in India.*

Sharma, Mridula (1996), "Privatization of Higher Education in India- Some Lessons from USA", *Journal of Higher Education*, Vol. 19, No. 3, pp. 375-399.

Singh, L.C. (2002-03), "Self-Financing Higher Education", *University News*, Vol. 40, No. 52, pp. 8-14.

Singh, R.P. (2004), "Higher Education: Who Should Finance", *University News*, Vol. 42, No. 06, Feb. 09-15, pp. 1-2.

Sinha, B.P. (1996), "Higher Education in Ancient India". In: Devendra Thakur and D.N. Thakur (eds), *Studies in Educational Development* Vol. 3 – *Higher Education and Employment,* Deep and Deep Publications, New Delhi, pp. 12-27.

Stella, Antony and Gnanam (2001), *Assessment and Accreditation in Indian Higher Education (Issues of Policy and Prospects),* Books Plus, New Delhi.

Sulochna (1993), "Financial Management of Higher Education in India", *Journal of Educational Planning and Administration*, Vol. VII, No. 1.

Swaminadhan, D. (1995), "IIigher Education Reforms-Financing, Freedom and Accountability", *Journal of Higher Education*, Vol. 18, No. 2, pp. 243-249.

Tan, Jee-Peng and Alain Mingat (1992), *Education in Asia-A Comparative Study of Cost and Financing.*

Tharu, Susie, *et al.* (1998), "Higher Education New Agendas, New Mandates", *Economic and Political Weekly,* October 17-24, pp. 2701-2702.

Tilak, J.B.G. (1987), *Cost of Education in Two Clusters in Harayana*, NIEPA, New Delhi.

Tilak, J.B.G. (1989), "Education and its Relation to Economic Growth, Poverty and Income- Past Evidence and Further Analysis", *World Bank Discussion Papers.*

Tilak, J.B.G., (1994), "External Financing of Education", *Journal of Educational Planning and Administration*, Vol. VIII, No. 1, Jan., pp. 81-86.

Tilak, J.B.G. (1995), "Cost Recovery Approaches in Education in India", Occasional Paper Series, NIEPA, New Delhi.

Tilak, J.B.G. (1995), "On Funding of Higher Education in India", *Journal of Higher Education*, Vol. 18, No. 2, pp. 291-300.

Tilak, J.B.G. (1996), "Unit Cost Analysis of Higher Education in India", in Devendra Thakur and D.N. Thakur (eds), *Studies in Educational Development* Vol. 3- *Higher Education and Employment*, Deep and Deep Publications, New Delhi, pp. 91-103.

Tilak, J.B.G. (1997), "Five Decades of Underinvestment in Education", *Economic and Political Weekly*, September 6, pp. 2239-2241.

Tilak, J.B.G. (1999), "National Human Development Initiative Education in the Union Budget", *Economic and Political Weekly*, March 6-13, pp. 614-620.

Tilak, J. B.G. (1999), "Student Loans as the Answer to Lack of Resources for Higher Education", *Economic and Political Weekly*, January 9.

Tilak, J.B.G. (2003), "Higher Education and Development in Asia", *University News*, Vol. XVII, No. 2, pp. 151-173.

Uberoi, N.K., (1995), "Higher Education: The Fate of Commissions and Committees — A lesson for Twenty First Century", *Journal of Higher Education*, Vol. 18, No. 3, pp. 485-494.

Umo, Joe U., (1980), "Production and Cost Functions for Higher Education in an LDC: The Nigerian Case", *Manpower Journal*, Vol. 16, No. 1, pp. 25-38.

Upadhye, Vidya V. (2003), "Higher Education Under the WTO Regime", *University News*, Vol. 41, No. 31, Aug. 04-10, pp. 6-11.

Varghese (1987), "Resources for Higher Education in India- An Explanation", *Journal of Higher Education*, Vol. 1, No. 3 and 4, July and October.

Varghese, N.V. (1991), "Management of Change in Higher Education- Some Trends", *Journal of Educational Planning and Administration*, Vol. V, No. 1, January, pp. 49-64.

Vilanilam, J.V. (1994), "The Economics of Higher Education: Implications of the Punnayya Committee Report for State Universities", *Journal of Higher Education*, Vol. 17, No. 2, 1994, pp. 239-249.

Welukar, Rajan M. and P.V. Page, V.M. Vaidya (2004), "Schemes for Fund Raising for Higher Education in India", *University News*, Vol. 42, No. 11, pp. 12-14.

World Bank (1985), *Management and Finance of Higher Education.*

Index

A

Age of the college, 55

Allowances, 117-120

Analysis of variance, 70

Arithmetic mean, 70

Arts and Science Colleges of Kerala, 55

B

Building, 138-139

C

Correlation, 70

Cost of college education in Punjab, 100-144

- allowances, 117-120
- broad analysis of the sample, 100-101
- building, 138-139
- composition of non-recurring funds, 142-143
- composition of output, 101-103
- equipment, 140-141
- furniture, 140
- library, 137-138
- nature of teaching staff, 103-107
- non-recurring expenditure, 135-137
- pattern of non-recurring expenditure and recovery, 143-144
- recovery of recurring cost from tuition fee, 131-133
- recurring cost analysis, 109-114
- recurring cost per unit, 120-121
- recurring cost recovery pattern, 127-129
- salary cost, 114-117
- selected correlates of unit cost, 122-127
- student-teacher ratio, 107-109
- surplus per unit, 133-135
- tuition fee and funds, 129-131

Cost of education, 59-70

- analytical tools, 70
- conceptualization of cost and its components, 60-63
- database of the study, 68
- institutional cost, 63
  - building, 64
  - chemicals and consumables, 67
  - equipment, 65
  - furniture, 66
  - games and sports, 65-66
  - hostel, 68
  - library, 64-65

salaries and allowances, 66-67
scholarships and stipends, 67
sample of the study, 68-70
Curriculum activities, 153

E

Education Commission (1966), 22, 44
Educational Development Bank, 52

F

Fifth Pay Commission, 81
Finance Commission, 16

G

GNP, 22
Gorakhpur University, 41
Graduate courses, 93-96

H

Higher education system in Punjab, 76-80, 83-87
Human capital, 144

I

Indian economy, 54
Institute of Correspondence Studies, 42
Institutions of higher education, 154
Introduction, 1-6
IT, 82

K

Liberalization, 2
Library, 137-138

M

Measurement issues
Anderson, 8
Padmanabhan, 7-8
Pandit, 6-7
Prakash, Shri, 8-9
Methodology, 3
Mobilization of Additional Resources for Technical Education, 31

N

Nehru, 17
Non-recurring expenditure, 135-137

O

Objectives, 3
Osmania University, 48

P

Planning Commission, 16
Policy implications, 155
Privatization, 2
Punjab, 100-144

R

Research Division of the World Bank Education and Training Department of World Bank, 17
Review of studies, 6-58

S

Salary cost, 114-117
Sixth Plan, 82
Smith, Adam, 22
State of Punjab, 156
Statistical Abstract of Punjab, 2005, 83
Structure of higher education in Punjab, 71-99
education and development, 72-73
graduate courses, 93-96

higher education system in Punjab, 83-87
Indian education system, 73-76
planned outlay on education in Punjab, 80-82
post-graduate education, 88-92
professional courses, 96-99
research related education, 87-88
structure of higher education in Punjab, 76-80
System-wise studies, 10
Dhesi, 33
Ghosh, 37
Jayaram, 21
Jena, 10
Majumdar, 16
Mathew, E.T., 32
Mehta, 25
Ramdas, 11
Shariff, 37
Tilak, 30
Vedagiri, 38
Verghese, 19

T

Taxation Inquiry Commission, 38
Teaching staff, 103-107
Tenth Five-Year Plan, 82
Tuition fee and funds, 129-131
Tuition fee, 154

U

UGC and State Government, 42
UGC report, 31
Unit cost of education, 39
Azad, 51
Datt, 40
Desai, 52
Dutt, 54
Ghuman, 53
Goel, 41
Gupta, 42
Kamat, 39
Mathew, 48
Padhi, 45
Panda, 45
Prakash, 42
Sahoo, 47
Salim, 55
Salim, 57
Sharma, 51
Sulochana, 48
Tilak, 43
Varghese, 49
Universities of the state, 148
University Grants Commission, 49
University of Delhi, 40
University of Rajasthan, 42
Urban area, 151